# The West Pole

The University of Minnesota Press gratefully acknowledges assistance provided for the publication of this volume by the John K. and Elsie Lampert Fesler Fund.

DIANE GLANCY

# The West Pole

UNIVERSITY OF
MINNESOTA PRESS
MINNEAPOLIS
LONDON

Published by the University of Minnesota Press
111 Third Avenue South, Suite 290
Minneapolis, MN 55401-2520

Printed in the United States of America on acid-free paper


Library of Congress Cataloging-in-Publication Data

Glancy, Diane
      The west pole / Diane Glancy.
            p.    cm.
      ISBN 0-8166-2894-7 (hardcover)
      1. Indians of North America—Literary collections. 2. Indians of North America—Civilization. 3. Women—Authorship.
      I. Title.
      PS3557.L294W47      1996
814'.54—dc20                                        96-36471

The University of Minnesota is an
equal-opportunity educator and employer.

But now they have a written language which can be easily written and read by even women and children.

*Reverend Nathaniel Burwash*
speaking of the Algonquins
1911

# Also by Diane Glancy

NOVELS
*Pushing the Bear* (1996)
*The Only Piece of Furniture in the House* (1996)

SHORT STORIES
*Monkey Secret* (1995)
*Firesticks* (1993)
*Trigger Dance* (1990)

ESSAYS
*Claiming Breath* (1992)

POETRY
*Boom Town* (1995)
*Coyote's Quodlibet* (1995)
*Lone Dog's Winter Count* (1991)
*Iron Woman* (1990)
*Offering* (1988)
*One Age in a Dream* (1986)

DRAMA
*War Cries* (1995)

ANTHOLOGIES
*Two Worlds Walking: Short Stories, Essays, and Poetry by Writers with Mixed Heritages,* edited by Diane Glancy and Bill Truesdale (1994)

# Contents

# Diffusionism

I remember long ago, after my first year at the University of Missouri, riding with my father to work. He got me a summer job in the stockyards. I wanted a typewriter and a watch, and in the Protestant work ethic we were now a part of, I would earn it. What I learned as I earned was that men had another world to live in. They could enter an *otherness* each day. My father was plant superintendent. I was a clerk in the order-supply office. But that summer there was more than my mother's boundary of housework and children. There was an occupation to be had.

I went back to school that fall, and later married and graduated and wrote and spent years with housework and children, but one day I put down my broom and looked out the window and there was *otherness* parked at the curb.

It came with a sense of writing. Which was the discovery of *The West Pole*. My father's way in the stockyards, the little he told me of our heritage, his failure to see my capacity, translated into story.

Or *storying*. The making of story.

Now, in the Native American tradition this is why Coyote is important: in a primitive culture where nothing is certain, where death and hunger are common, and survival is tenuous, Coyote appears. Now I was beyond the tenuous business. Established you might say. Around for a while. But it was the same survival urge. The migration to *otherness*.

You know Coyote, no matter what he did or how hard he did it, ended up with nothing. Yet he lives and prevails. Well. In the style of Coyote, you create story. An illusion of reality. You move from one illusion to another. Images arise and in the act of imaging you create a reality. Not the images you make. Because they disappear. But the process of making. The energy force you create that transcends the nothing that Coyote always has. So in creating, you *story* a life force in which there is existence independent of the reality of hunger, fear, disease, death, and the inexplicable happenings.

In storying more images come. You have transcended by the process of remaking.

That's what migration was about, I guess. Often the Native people covered the same trails from summer to winter camp. The same herds had their patterns too. But in the agency of travel was renewal. That's also *The West Pole*. The collective, *multiform* monologues about writing, teaching, lecturing, relationships, traveling, and starting up in different places and times. The journey over the same trails toward *Being*. The vital trip to *otherness*. A traveling in which you develop a center. Until you know wherever you are is the center of the earth.

I'm not a Plains Indian, yet I find myself writing in those terms at first. I grew up in Kansas City on the edge of the plains. But I'm from a sedentary Woodland tribe, the Cherokee, and only a part of it. After my great-grandfather left Indian Territory, he settled in northern Arkansas and farmed. It was almost fifty years later, when my father left for the stockyards in Kansas City, that the family "migrated."

But the uncertainty of my displaced part-Indian, part-white, mixed-message heritage is in the Diffusionist Theory, in a way. Civilization began in many different places, in different times, in different ways. Not just one. Otherwise a stasis in its unmoving certainty.

I had no clear image of myself as a Native person. I was a part-Cherokee living on land that had belonged to another tribe. I didn't have much knowledge of "Indians" other than the headband and feather we made at Thanksgiving at school in Kansas City. And my father's ways, which were different from others around me.

That's what this book is about: a *reconstructing* of *voice* blended so thoroughly it's almost lost. Yet the "Indian voice" is one that speaks with presence. As a Cherokee, I knew about Sequoyah. A mixed-blood who made the Cherokee syllabary in the 1820s. I can't read Cherokee, of course. But the point is, with the written language that he called "talking leaves," he gave the people a way to "*story*": a way to record the "migration" as they struggled across the moving landscape of their lives.

*The West Pole* is about the expanding and differing definitions of the term. It's about culture and our struggle to survive both personal and historic desolation.

3

NOW

# Hides

I can't say I'm of the bear clan or the elk people.
Just a man who came north for work
and left all that.

I have been questioned as a white.
I have been questioned as Indian.
I am neither of both worlds.
But one of my own making.
Mainly by words.

I speak with a mixed voice.
An acculturated voice.
Because my Indian heritage was picked off.
I remember the smallpox vaccination scab on my arm.
Picking it off.
And it dropping to the ground.
I remember picking it up.
Trying to stick it back on.

Anyway.

• • •

I guess you want to hear about the land. And how the Indian
ancestors followed the buffalo. And how the sky spoke to them
in the smoke signals of its clouds. And how the rocks were
known to turn and speak the way you're walking with someone somewhere and they say something you know right then
you'll remember all your life. But you know it isn't that way.
Though I know a rock. The weight of it in my hand like a
heart. Sometimes I hold it to my ear and say, hey rock—how

you? And I know the open prairie where you drive for days and still don't see the end. You go on forever and know nothing except a few cafés and a room for the night. You know my father asked me if I wanted some animal hides. He worked for the stockyards and could get them for me. But I didn't know what to do. Whad he expect? Moccasins and dresses? A reconstruction of the drum? Where would I get the heartbeat? After the earth was paved and covered with the rattle of cattle trucks. But you know. I guess you can hear anything again. You can still scrape hides. If only through the imagination in your own head.

# Who Can Speak as an Indian?

The issue makes me *squirm*. My great-grandfather was Cherokee. My grandmother probably half. My father a fourth. Me an eighth. I could be more but I'm not sure.

But what part's Indian? My feet? My hands?

No—I think it's a voice in my chest. I hear it among the other voices. Late at night when the dish of scraps is set out back. Under the heavy trees in the distance where we used to drive to Arkansas. Not many times, but enough.

The Indian voice speaks with my hands. I guess it's my pencil that's Indian. And didn't my red school tablet say *Big Chief*?

It was Sequoyah who made the Cherokee syllabary so the people could write. Working with the alphabet is like driving a car. I get transported to a lot of places. My broken voice rides a broken vehicle. I use a mixed-story format. I assimilate "story."

That Indian part is a memory I have. An anger over something that's gone. I don't have what I ought to know: There's a story I'll call "The Nose Eaters."

• • •

*I remember hearing about a grandmother who got her granddaughter out of the hospital. She was a Dakota, I think. This was after relocation. The girl had cut her nose and needed stitches. Maybe she had fallen. But the grandmother went to the hospital and got her, and took her home and healed her somehow.*

• • •

That's what I missed. The healing ceremony. The connection to that power. As a girl, I cut my nose when I fell, and was wrapped in a sheet until I couldn't move. I think of the needle

9

entering my skin when the doctor took stitches. Yes, I think it felt like he was eating my nose.

How many heritages do I draw from? Even my last name is something I am not. It belongs to an Irishman I was married to.

But isn't "fragment" the tune of the day? Are all Indians Dakota? Are all Cheyenne? Are all full-bloods? Are all traditional or assimilated? Can all walk together even in the same family?

And how about the Christianity the family was converted to? How many tribes in it? For some, you have to be a member of their denomination to go to heaven. For others, you have to accept Christ as savior and be born again. For still others, you have only the fellowship of the congregation and the example of Jesus you should try to follow. There are other possibilities. I sometimes think of Jesus as a living spirit, a *story*, in other words. To give strength and *re-formation* along the migration trail.

Which ensures, at least, I have words when I have nothing else.

# Genealogy

I was not raised in the traditional way, and you can ask what right have I got to speak? But the Native American voice is the one I hear when I write.

My father's people were Cherokee. I remember him telling me we were Indian. I remember asking, what kind? My great-grandfather, Woods Lewis, was born in 1843 near Sallisaw, Oklahoma. His name was *Paskwals* or *Pasqua* before he changed it. That's the fragment I have from his granddaughter, my aunt. He got in trouble just before the Civil War and fled Oklahoma Territory. After serving in Company L, Fourth Tennessee Cavalry, he tried to return to Oklahoma, which was still Indian Territory at the time, but word got out, and he had to settle in northern Arkansas, where he farmed until his death in 1904.

My father went north to Kansas City to work in the stockyards just before the Depression. He buried his heritage as my great-grandfather, and my grandmother, had done. He married a German-English woman and I was raised in the white culture knowing little of my father's heritage. But even in the white schools and churches I attended, I was always asked the inevitable question by teachers. What nationality was I?

They knew I was something other, but they weren't sure what.

In some of us, the heritage has been rendered nearly invisible. At least unrecognizable. The voice can't be seen anyway. But I felt it moving in me for years, and it finally found visibility in the written word.

I think I speak for a lot of Native Americans who have mixed blood and who know little of their culture and language. But the heritage shows up now and then like the Indian ancestors, whom I know sometimes, when I wake in the morning, have been there in the night.

# School

Invisibility was the first clue I was different.
Maybe it's why my father told me we were Indian. Maybe I
had felt my difference and asked.

In grade school, I remember not counting. Nothing was ever
asked of me other than to repeat lessons. Other than being tol-
erated. Who was I, anyway?

I passed through the early years of school waiting. That's
what I learned.

Then in high school. I faced it first-hand. The behavior from
the undervalued self. I started smoking. Drinking. There was
promiscuity.

But then I was small and dark and attractive to boys. That's
the core of thought. The way it felt when they touched me. It's
what they wanted. I let them. It was nearly forty years ago.
There's safety in that.

And the shyness. I remember once having to give a panel report in class. Civics, maybe. It was the result of a semester pro-
ject. I refused to speak. In spite of the teacher's threats and
admonitions, I refused. Later she dismissed the class and I
never gave the report.

In college, I could hardly take an exam because of the fear. It
took me five years to get through. Another twenty-four before
I went back for an M.F.A.

It took that long to find the ability to function in school.
It took that long to find my permission to exist.
To lose a self turned against itself.

. . .

It took even longer to find out I could do what I do.

But to be on the outside is to know you were from someplace else. No one would talk about it though. Or explain it. I was just something that didn't fit. I could have been part of the white world. Yes. Except for the heart.

# Sometimes I Lose It

I had a Lakota man speak to my Native American literature class. He said when you're made to feel different from everyone, it messes you up. His voice was a stick poking the animal from underneath the porch of my heart. The years of darkness. Isolation. I felt the abrupt change in my chest. The animal jerking away from the stick. Its spasms near my heart. Tears rising to my eyes in front of the students. The terror of my own years. The difference felt. The unyielding fight.

# PARTS OF THREE LECTURES

# Comment

I write the sections of my life as a whole. Not separated into several books but moving in one book from one part toward another. Changing subjects too soon. Always in transit too fast between the critical and the personal. Traveling for a reading. Returning to the classroom. Late to one meeting in one place. Another in another. Too many demands. Afterward sitting at my desk with my cat on my lap. Trying to pick up where I was. Grading papers through a weekend. Trying to catch up with reading. Sometimes a movie on Friday nights.

These three lectures were given at (1) Northland College in Wisconsin where I remember driving through the pines on a narrow northern Wisconsin road to get there, (2) the Loft in Minneapolis on a cold winter Saturday morning, and (3) the Midwest Modern Language Association Chicago I remember flying to give.

# Culture and Environment: Voices in the Wind

I want to present another element, or dimension of land.
Land as words.
As voices.
As storytelling.

Words have bodies and spirits.
Bodies are the written parts.
Spirits are the meaning that enter the ear and form
the head's landscape—
a landscape of understanding, meaning, feeling, thought,
idea. In other words—the concepts that inform our actions.

We are made of words. The words we speak are what we are.

I think landscape also has the two parts:
the physicality of it—
the trees and grass and crops, et cetera
but there's also a message—a meaning, an energy force,
a living being that the earth is.
And we are not separate from it.
In fact, according to Genesis and some of the Native
American myths, we are made from it.
Its very being is the source and substance of our bodies. We
come from it and return to it. We also interact with it during
our stay on it.

*Why all this landscape description?* My students ask in reading
the novels in my NA lit course. *Let's get on with it—the plot,
conflict, the important stuff.*

But landscape is a person, a character, in Native American lit, not the setting.

In fact, sometimes landscape actually tells the story.
If you want to know what's going on in the story
read the imagery of the landscape.

We've lost so much of our connection to the land in Western culture. Except for farmers who have known the fields all their lives.

Now what if the land is also made of words
since it is also a living being?

$$\cdots$$

Isn't it in Genesis that God spoke the world into being? If the land is made of words, couldn't you hear them if you listened?

$$\cdots$$

There's also a story in the Native American tradition of how the Great Spirit spoke the world into being. At one time he was lonely, you see, because that's the way it is when you're the Great Spirit without anyone like yourself to talk to. So he made the elements. He said *Tree, you be a tree and stand there on the land. Hill, you be a hill.* And so forth. But the Great Spirit was still lonely, even after all that. Because the wind could make some noise, but there was still no one to really talk to. So he made the animals. The buffalo snorted. The wolf howled. But the Great Spirit longed for something more. So he made man. Just spoke him into being. (Though in other versions, we came from other places.) (Because that's the nature of story. To offer options. So we can have choices. So there'll be alternatives.) Because that's why the Spirit made us. With free wills and minds of our own. So we could be independent agents. So we could offer him some options. Because that's what you've got to have for conversation. For being *not lonely*. Which was the reason for our creation. So we could talk to the Great

Spirit. Be a companion. Cause him a little trouble so he could use his *peacemaker* talents.

. . .

But the point I've been trying to get to:
Since we have a voice, maybe the land also has a voice.
I hear the land sometimes, just as I hear my father's voice once in a while, and he's been gone twenty years.

It's not a voice you hear with the ears, but in the inner self, you hear it speaking. (It says to live with resilience and dignity, with variable patterns and cycles mixed at times with change and disruption. It tells me I live because it does.) It also confirms a sense of life-force or power. I often write from that voice.

It's a practical sense that there's more to it than we know. Not in an escapist, romantic, or pastoral way but in a practical sense of what's going on.

I come from a Cherokee father and a German-English mother whose parents farmed in Kansas all their lives. I think some of my writing is an attempt to keep those ties to the land.
To record some of the stories of the land so I don't forget my responsibility.

For instance, in the story of the origin of corn in the Cherokee myth, Selu, a woman, was killed, and where her blood fell, the corn grew.
Much as in the Christian sense of new life coming from the blood of Christ.
To be informed of both cultures often helps me walk in both worlds.

To put my ear to the earth until I could hear the heart (which is what the drumbeat means in Indian ceremony, in the pow wow). A heartbeat, which indicates life.

As a writer, I can drive out into the land and hear it. In the years I was traveling for the arts council in Oklahoma, I drove out to the land after school.
It was a friend when there was no one else.
Part of its job is to be a companion to me.
To share its words. To be worth its creation.
Maybe the same is true for me, since reciprocity is a principle of life in the Native American tradition.

I think what I feel is the opposite of *anthropomorphism*.
It may be the other way around—what if qualities that are really the earth's are attributed to us?

I wonder if the earth also has feelings
and if our feelings were first felt by the earth?

It may be nature that has the feelings and we're something like it in our ability to feel.

Now, the Bible talks about the importance of the land, yet with a different outcome.
The Bible says we come from the land and return to it.
But the difference: "Cursed is the ground for your sake; in sorrow you shall eat of it all the days of your life. Thorns also and thistles shall it bring forth. In the sweat of your face you shall eat bread until you return to the ground, for out of it you were taken, for dust you are, and unto dust you will return." Genesis 3:17-19

That's a heavy punishment.
It broke harmony, it caused the death of a vital link. The oneness of land and human beings.

It's also one of the differences between Native culture and Christianity.

In Native culture, we are the land. It's a vital part of our definition. But according to Christianity, we have to live separate from our source.

In those terms, the curse of the ground was even more serious than we realize. Not only are we cut off from God, the father, but also the land, our mother.
We live as orphans.
Or we are here to fight the land. Like a family turned against itself.

("Cursed for our sake"—is interesting, by the way—as though we gain something by having to struggle to get back to, to be reunited with. Earth is now our enemy—for our sake, for our benefit.
Maybe in experiencing the land as an enemy, we realize it is another being with a mind of its own, just like us.)

Sometimes I also feel the captivity of the earth,
or she lets herself be for us,
like a mother who stays home for her children.

I'm only trying to walk in both worlds. They don't go together. But incongruity and paradox are a part of life.

I am assimilated, yet I can't turn my back to the world that part of my heritage knew in such a different way.

The earth has a story to tell. And we'd better listen. Harmony and reciprocity are the principles for our survival. The land is our being. To pollute it is to pollute ourselves.

The eighteenth chapter of Leviticus (verses 25–28) states that the earth can "spew" us out if it wants.

Nature came first in all creation accounts, then animals, and lastly us. We should not be ignorant of these matters.

In our conversation, we should honor the land as an elder, as a living entity. Remember it has dignity and existence just as we do. In fact, it had them first.

How we treat it is how we treat ourselves. It's how we become a true human being.

Our idea of land is central to ourselves.

We come into unity with ourselves in our concept of land.

# Their Eyes Have Seen the Buffalo

My students are sometimes disappointed in the first classes of Native American literature. They want an immediate spirituality. And the characters in the books are lost. They suffer from alcoholism, posttraumatic stress syndrome, dependency, brokenness, purposelessness, and numerous other ailments. One character believes he is invisible. Another is inarticulate. Still another doesn't seem to have a name. But in their cruel and absurd lives, there are possibilities of ceremonies. One of the strongest is the love the characters find in the faulty little medicine bag of the human heart.

What's going on here? The students ask. This isn't what I wanted. Where are the chiefs and holy men who talk like Chiefs Joseph and Seattle? Where are the medicine women who sew ghost shirts as a shield against bullets so the warriors can ride into battle and not be shot?

There seems to be some disappointment that Indians are usually ordinary people. Are all whites ministers and presidents? Aren't there many levels of social strata in all cultures?

I think spirituality eventually comes, but not in the direct way the students expect. It's respectful not to look someone in the eye. Maybe truth also comes indirectly.

Sometimes I think I hear the spirits. I think mostly I hear them laugh because they have lots of things going on other than us. Yes. I think we make them sad. I don't hear them with my ears of course. That's not where you hear things like that. I think angels before they get promotion in heaven have to live with Indians on earth. I think they have to know how to be wiped out. How to give life to words again by speaking them.

You see, you can say something from the spirit world without someone knowing what you're doing. They have to first learn to listen. The spirit world protects itself. I wish I knew what I know is going on sometimes. But I'm preoccupied or who knows what. Whatever I do, or don't do, doesn't change the spirit world anyway. It goes on whether I see it or not.

Native American literature can be frustrating at first. Especially those who come to it with *unit* thinking and do not like the erasure of boundaries, the group effort, I suppose. The relaxing of borders. The gathering of many voices. The circular form rather than the establishment of a power structure.

Say that everyone in the family goes to a pow wow. Everyone comes home. Around the table everyone tells their version of it, until the one pow wow becomes the many versions and the moving reality is the pow wow. The text of authority is everyone's opinion since there are many ways of seeing and experiencing.

But I guess linear thinking has its purpose. America achieved civilization and technology, and wouldn't the world be in trouble without its generosity? And the Native American has it too. The electronic beadwork of casino machines is one of the names of it. So the demarcation lines are not simplistic. But to generalize. To start from a simple point of departure for the trail of the talk into the morning.

I think Native American novels are about how to live without the heart. Or only the ghost of it. As one lives with the ancestors. Mostly by faith. Though you hear them. When you're driving through an ice storm trying to get back to Minnesota after Thanksgiving break, for instance. Or when you wake in the morning sometimes you know they've been there maybe sitting on the edge of the bed trying to be quiet. You know they're looking through your books shaking their heads at what you've been reading. Maybe being startled when the phone rings and wishing for smoke signals again. Or they're

27

holding your car keys talking about what it would be like to drive.

I was raised at some distance from my Cherokee heritage. We made frequent trips to visit my mother's parents' farm in Kansas, but we rarely went to northwest Arkansas. It's where my father's mother lived in Viola, just under the Missouri border. I remember crossing Norfolk Lake in our car on the ferry. I remember a tall and bony woman with a long face and coarse gray hair. Not entirely white. Not entirely Indian. Especially not the image I had of the Plains Indian with a teepee and buffalo. My father's mother had a row of corn and some pigs. But in that water crossing, there was entry into an old world of mystery and little-people tales and a certain discomfort. My father's mother died when I was eleven. Before I could know to ask her what I later wanted to know.

Many Native Americans are raised with that distance. At conferences all the time I hear them speak about how they are cut off from their heritage. How they don't speak their language. Not all of them. But too many. My Native heritage is a special faraway world in which rocks and trees speak and the ancestors come sometimes for supper. And I've known them many nights alone on the road when I had to travel. They were there beside the highway riding their spirit horses. Migrating with me though the Cherokee didn't migrate, but in the northern areas it is the indigenous tribes that come. I have a distinct voice in my head. An old Indian somewhere out on the land. Probably Nebraska. It's the voice I write from sometimes. We are all one. There is no distance or separation though we are separate. I'm speaking here of the Human Being. *Ani-yun-wiyu.* Those Human Beings with the capital *H* and *B*. It's one's own choice, as to what kind you are. The real Human Beings are the hard ones to be. Sometimes to get through life you have to pack your heart in tobacco and walk on. Though it may be a way you don't want to go. To this day when I go to pow wows

I feel that emptiness that comes back. The something I had that wasn't there. Life as a present under the tree you opened and found the box empty. But at least you have the box in which something came. You could spend your life reconstructing what was erased. Erasure. The point of deconstruction. The Native American had that done to our lives. Probably others too. I think that's why students take NA lit. They're looking for what belongs in the empty box. And they don't find easy answers, but a complex set of books in which they must face the darkness. Put it on as if it were a coat. Cover themselves with the soot and dust of the earth and run through the dark until with sweat it is washed off, and the dawn rises finding them nearly clean. Or tell their story. Find the half-breed Mexican cattle that an uncle lost. Forgo evil. Reverge. Avoid it. Or face nothingness and endure it. Or build a bridge with butter knives over water glasses in a bar in Fargo, North Dakota, and stand on an empty space midriver and say *There's a bridge here,* and walk as though they felt the concrete under their feet.

Re-image.

Re-imagine.

Find new words.

Verb and reverb. All over the place.

I was not raised with the culture, and even if I had been, it would be different from the books I teach. There's a vast range in Native American culture. All tribes have a differing and generous supply of creation myths and explanation tales, spiritual beliefs and spirits. Never ending. On and on. Some of them are basic. Where we came from, how we got here, and what do we do once we're here. What the world is like. How we should behave. What we have found to believe.

My father was first a practical man. He took his spiritualism in the form of church on Sunday mornings. My father's ceremony was responsibility. I'm grateful for it. I remember in the early days when he'd hunt and bring back the rabbit and quail to the basement floor. Something was there in the act of knifing buckshot from the bird or animal. In the skinning. Dressing. I remember our ritual as I squatted beside him. Something unspoken passed. A respect for life. Getting to work in the morning. Coming home at night to his family. An example. A man of this world. He started from nothing and became plant superintendent of Armour's. That's the Native American hero to me.

It's not history nor spiritual vision quest, though those things may come.

When I look at the memories of my grandmother, the words that still spill from her somehow, I get an overwhelming sadness. How do I live responsibly in a world I do not feel a part of, and through which I can pass invisibly? How do I live when I don't want to? With suicide and drugged forgetfulness? How do I live with the nothingness that most of the white culture also has at its core?

Besides sadness, I feel mostly paradox. The terrible strength of my heritage. I felt it last the day after Thanksgiving driving back from Kansas City. There was heavy fog in northern Iowa. Then ice and finally snow in Minnesota. Possibly sixteen inches when the old twenty-eight-incher was still on the ground. I didn't expect it. I had watched a weather map on the news before I left Kansas City and there was a snowflake over Minnesota. But there always is. November through April. The oncoming traffic lighted the trees beside the highway, which glistened with ice like ghosts of the ancestors and elders saying *Drive on*. That's what they say. All the time I ask for wisdom. I get the same answer. *Keep going*. Flagmen, they think they are.

Then the shame I remember. All characters in the novels deal with it. My mother was not happy with my father's Indian heritage. She disliked the meat my father hunted and anything else connected to that way of life. She didn't mention it. Hardly ever. She didn't have to. Silently I knew what we were.

I think this *walking-in-two-worlds* business is really in my own Native culture. Instead of one foot in the white world and one in the Indian. Maybe I need three feet to explain this. One in the white world and two in the Indian. There's the ideal Indian you see. The spiritual one who used to be. And there's also the new Indian. Who has lost his heritage and lives in a fragmented social structure. Who pulls others down. It's the big shots who go to college. The rest live on commodities and first-of-the-month welfare checks. Dependency is the epidemic.

I also think of the nuns and priests who beat the Indian children in boarding schools. They had not been raised with discipline. They were stubborn and hardheaded. Still are. Rebellious. With a tendency sometimes to delinquent behavior. The Indians must have driven the nuns and priests to drink themselves. But that's no excuse for what they did to the Indian children. At conferences I've heard Indians who were in those schools talk. Sixty years can pass and the emotion is almost still unbearable. You can hear the beatings in their voices. In the name of religion those-who-came muddied the waters for many Indians. They turned Christianity sour forever for most who went through that system.

But I'll tell you what I think. And many Native Americans don't want to hear. I think the Native American is pretty much like any human being who had a high culture built on codes of honor and a behavior and way of life that were in harmony with their existence. Except the Native American had the unique experience of losing his land and way of life, which for the northern Plains culture was bound up in the buffalo as food source and really life-force. And facing nothing, the Indian found that human codes of honor, that ritual and ceremonies, that ideas of dignity and strength mostly do not survive the stripping of culture and way of life in which those ideas existed. And that the human being is naked not only physically but also emotionally. We are a vacuum that needs to be filled. I think so anyway. And it's what the Native American novels seem to say.

My *filling* anyway has been in the Someone who came and acted out the Ceremonies. For me it is Christ. Did not Mountain Wolf Woman see him in her peyote visions? Did not Black Elk talk of him in the Ghost Dance visions? The one who still Sun Danced when human fabric failed? Not certainly in the religion that the priests and nuns brought with cruelty in the name of *saving souls*. But in the life-force of Christ. The True Buffalo. The One Who Danced on the Cross. Who was the final Sun Dancer. The Spirit who did for me what I could not do on my own. Which is to survive darkness. And in turn he gave me the power to drive through darkness without any other help than his. I am sharing what I have found to be true for my life. Which is the buffalo my eyes have seen. Which is what Native American novels talk about in the end.

They expel you from themselves to form your own story. When I am alone and in need, I tell a story and it gives me a spiritual energy to go on.

I think even machines have stories. Once, as I listened to the snowblower across the street, I heard the sound of a motorboat far out on the lake. It spoke to my memory of the lake. The sound of the snowblower hummed with story and old summers at my uncle's cabin on the Lake of the Ozarks in Missouri when I was young and had the morning to do what I liked. Maybe the snowblower can't be eaten like a sled dog or scent its way home, but it has a new-age spirit and it does the job.

In conclusion, all storytelling says that we began in chaos and forever make cover for the waters over which we exist. And that migration trails still have to be walked. Because in migration one becomes strong. That's the point of migration. Not just to have somewhere to go. But to see the buffalo. Except there aren't many to see except in national parks in South Dakota or Montana or on the small buffalo farm at the truck stop beside Turner Turnpike in Oklahoma. But when my eyes have seen them, I recognize them as Other. As something beyond the grasp of self.

That's the insight. Context. Interpretation of Native American literature.

The way I see it anyway.

# Washing out the War-Clothes

Now this is a Lakota War Song
hoksila ki   sukawakan a' opta o pelo
boy   the horse   on his   shot

phehi huska ki   kuwa
hair   long   the   chase

It means *The young warrior (was) killed by longhairs (soldiers)
who chased him*

(translated by Violet Brown, Newberry Library, Chicago)

• • •

which means
(1) the soldiers were doing the chasing
(2) it was a fast chase since the hair flew out behind
(3) since long hair represents strength
    in other words it's an invocation for
(4) the strength that comes through the doing

• • •

This late-nineteenth-century song-for-revenge was chanted
until the warriors had courage to ride into a column of soldiers
outnumbered and outweaponed. The repetition of the words
over and over produced a trancelike state in which a spiritual
strength transcended the limits of common sense.

You know they say when the Indian first saw a man on a
horse he didn't know they were separate. No. The white man—
the Spanish conquistador really—brought the horse to the
South, then the North American continent. The Indian probably didn't have a horse before that, though some say he did. Be-

cause of some horse bones they found. Because of some horse-maker story.

When the Native American lost his language he lost his order of seeing because there was a split between the riding over the ground on which there was riding.

If you want to conquer a people. Take their language, which is their way of thinking, their carrier-of-culture-and-meaning, their sense-of-being. Send them on a long trail to another place. Mow them down with soldiers. Wipe out the buffalo.

But can you imagine America remaining in its wilderness while the rest of the world moved on? With all the natural resources. Ore and copper. The ground and air. The peacemaker's blessing. Well the Indian had to find out he wasn't the only one. And America has fed the world. Said *ho* to the wagons. Reached the West Pole. Looked for a while as though it invented the rest of the earth. Or Elm Street anyway. The row of them over all American streets until disease felled the canopy of sameness. The whole lack of diversity. The melting pot taking out now what doesn't melt.

• • •

I'm shooting my arrow into the text, you see.
Making a reservation of it.
So you know how it feels.
Separating the horse from the rider.
In other words, hair long can define a chase.

In Minnesota I heard this name. Chief Hole-in-the-Day.
I think it's him
through which meaning leaves the rebellion
of the shrinking text. The pillow
cases of soda pop on the back porch.
The codefendants of the meaning's words.

Native American genres sometimes de-genre-ate. Because no one dominant understanding emerges from the Native

American essay. Possibly no one thematic statement, development, or conclusion. No apparent motive. Not even a recognizable point of departure, destination, or arrival.

And all of it with the pastoral transcendence
of a buffalo jump.
Not with beginning or end.
But simply the process. The experience of the journey.
The extended movement across the plains
without section lines separating the voices.
But all getting a chance you see.

If I were to write a Native American essay, of course. To be aware of different possibilities in ways-of-seeing. Maybe that's Native American theory and practice. A voice against monoculture.

Furthermore if language is fair game for itself
if it is seen as kinetic
everchanging and moving
not so much toward destination
but migration for the sake of renewal and transformation
in the journey
words stick together or get misunderstood or misinterrupted.
Old spellings dissolve.
One sees the residue of language and puts it together
in new ways of untried versions.
Always naming and renaming.
The word to truth is first a dirt road you know.
I'm trying to say language is in flux
as in a game reserve
the wolves \ buffalo \ longhorns not always
in their proper bins but wherever glad to be with.
· · ·

You know there are stories that can only be told when it snows. Possibly because when it's clear you're supposed to be doing other things. (1) Getting ready for winter, for instance. (2) The spirits that accompany the stories are only around in winter. Spending the cold months south I suppose. (3) In winter concentration is high because there's not much else to do, which invites stories into one's being where they are carried for those-who-come-after.

To hear the voices that have been left out by the edict of a choice voice. Because they had the power to suppress. A this is it. No other way than our own. A life in school that wasn't there when I remember what it was like. Which was to endure the nothing that happened. And the only trip home was a story on the way. Like a conversion is the hearing other voices. Reaching other shores and claiming it belongs to others. So let it be.

. . .

But identifying others threatens one's own.
Holding the language in discomfort.
Otherwise the grim reckoning by the left-out voice.
You have to pack up your heart and walk through it
knowing the aloneness.

. . .

Yes, Native American practice and theory is a loosening of the authority of the canon. A step to the commonality of a few more things. A check-and-balance system after all.

NOW

# Late in the Afternoon

I was talking with him at the kitchen table. About my father
and how when he was alive I felt someone else was in the
world with me. And my friend said how he would go home
after school and his mother would hold him on her lap. I knew
she had died when he was nine. It was one of those families,
you know. That didn't work. But it wasn't that. Most of them
don't. I guess. But I could feel his mother's love around him.
And she'd been dead fifty years. It doesn't mean anything.
Time that is. Maybe that's the point. We talk about it mostly.
But that afternoon we were in my kitchen. And I was on my
friend's lap instead of him on his mother's. But it was the same.
Those times after school when two people connect and hold
one another. And maybe he and his mother would have toast
and some strong tea. The table had papers on it. The clutter of
mail and books that would have to be cleared for supper. And
now in my small kitchen, I tell him how wrinkling a piece of
tinfoil, I remember the sound of sleet on the kitchen window.
Maybe my mother was wrapping a sandwich for my lunch box
or covering brownies and she was never happy about it. Unlike
his. It's the sound that silence would have if it had sound. Before something begins that you have to do and you feel yourself quivering with invisibility. Or when you hear others talk
and know they live in a world that has no place for you and
you are without significance. Maybe the past closes you out.
And you think how it's getting close to winter outside. In the
small kitchen someday you'll hear sleet on the window. And
you'll remember the sandwich wrapped in tinfoil before
school. And you think how you live over fifty years before you
realize how much like tinfoil that sleet can sound.

# The Chart of Elements

For a moment we were wag-tailed. I felt the fragile lift of the human heart. As it lumbered into air. Suddenly there were branches. Yo. In the University of Minnesota Katherine Nash Gallery. I went there to speak on Native American historical perspectives. In the West Bank Union auditorium next to the gallery. But you know on your way to one thing you find another. Twig art. Woodwork. Branches twisted into ladders. Small bridges across the heart.

# The Germany Trip

5/19–6/4
*Home Abroad–Abroad Home*
Writers' conference in Freiburg
and a five-city reading tour

*for Jay Moon*

5/19 4:30 P.M. flight Minneapolis/St. Paul–Chicago

My companion's birthday after an argument over him having his birthday lunch with his sons and former wife. What did they get divorced for? But he still goes. It was more than an argument. I gave away his cake. A colleague's husband died. An artist who was also a window washer, he fell from the Carlson Towers in Minneapolis. He had illustrated one of my poetry books. And I took the cake to her.

It isn't ever what we think it will be—reaching high while falling back to earth.

The plane feels rough on the running. My writing goes wild. The ponds and lakes look ruffed from the air, and I don't remember wind. How do you love someone again after a long and difficult marriage? How do you reach? But once you're up over the edge of the city, the squared-off country lines up its lunch boxes. Their order finally on this shaky trip. After I behaved at best sixth grade. I get angry easily now. I gave up tolerance after marriage. I will have it my way or no way now. Maybe an attitude adjustment will occur. Some miracle by lighting a candle in some cathedral in Germany. Or maybe somewhere I'll touch an angel and be renewed with patience.

My companion, Jack, will come back a week early because the university is on quarters. But at my college I turned in my grades before I left, hurrying through final short stories and scripts from two classes. I wrote to a few students who were graduating. Earlier I rushed for a passport. Now it's traveler's checks in German and a Eurail pass. Leaving the house in order. Finding someone to feed the cat and mow the lawn.

My watch didn't get repaired in time, though it was in the shop two weeks. The stem on back order. I told them I wasn't happy. At Target, I bought a Minnie Mouse watch. It was really Mickey that first caught my eye, but once I moved down the counter and saw her in her red polka-dot skirt and red hat with flower and her wide yellow pumps and yellow gloves moving as if directing planes to their gate, I knew it was her.

Now over Wisconsin I look at my companion reading *Say It in German Phrase Book for Travelers*. We cross the Mississippi maybe at the confluence of Iowa, Wisconsin, and Illinois.

There had been a reserve in the car as his son drove us to the airport. I had behaved badly over the birthday lunch. I felt replaced, I guess, and had canceled a birthday dinner I was going to have for him. Anything I said seemed to say I had been a jerk. You see, you don't really grow up no matter how old you get. That's the secret. I'm letting you in on it now so you can get rid of that weight of hope.

Thirty-five minutes into the short flight from Minneapolis/ St. Paul to Chicago, I feel the plane start to go down. I'm looking in the airline's magazine at a huge wood angel the color of apple juice. Its mouth set in some sort of pout over Buenos Aires, I guess.

Jack writes down information. We'll arrive at gate C. He looks at the tickets for our connecting flight. He looks in the airline magazine for the other terminal. I don't write down anything because I'm with a man. I don't have to think. Simply follow. A habit I had with my former husband that quickly kicked in. That was hard after the divorce. Finding my own way through airports. Somewhere on board, there's an unhappy child. The captain tells us we've got forty-seven miles left in our descent to Chicago. I watch from the window as we fall, not the way a man falls from a building, but slowly sliding back to earth.

I follow Jack through the Chicago airport, at first as bright with glass as angel wings. We walk from terminal to terminal, down the escalator, up. Then through a corridor, down an elevator, into a tunnel, and across a moving walkway to another terminal. When we reach our gate for the overseas carrier, my hand is shaking from pulling my heavy carry-on bag on wheels. I'd even found time to go to the bookstore one last time before leaving to buy a few books I want to catch up on. I even had time to find the old genealogy of my mother's maternal, German side of the family that I knew was somewhere in the stacks of papers in my study.

When I look at the crowd in this out-of-the-way terminal, I feel the impact of Europeans returning to Europe—people looking different from Americans, speaking differently. They are mostly stockier, dressed in clothes from another decade. The plane is crowded. There's noise and heat and the movement of storing sacks and bags and small luggage. It must already feel like a European marketplace. We sit in our tight seats. *Tell me you're glad you came,* I say, and he says he's glad.

Jack is the first man I've traveled with, with whom I've been in love. By the time my former husband and I were on the travel circuit for his job, we were longing for the next step in our lives away from the problems of the other.

I listen to the multilingual greetings from the captain.

There's an eight-and-a-half-hour, 4,435-mile flight from Chicago to Zurich. We back from the gate, wait, then soon there's a loud roar, a slight shift in cargo, and a squeak of wheels as they retract. We're already crossing the Great Lakes, heading toward Canada, then east across the Atlantic. What will I do all night in this small seat? Sit beside him in a fizz of sleeplessness. My legs aching to be up. Eight hours and fifteen minutes to go.

Ground speed is 478 miles an hour. There's the world's weather map on the monitor above our heads in the crowded cabin. I can track temperatures from Santiago to Europe if I want. I can watch our plane fly up the St. Lawrence River and out across the ocean to Ireland. The earth has suddenly opened like my old dining room table with all its leaves.

I look from my small window. The earth and sky are streaked purple with evening. Dinner comes and Jack explains the difference between kilometers and miles—*A kilometer is .62 mile*, he says. For the difference between Celsius and Fahrenheit, *subtract 32 and divide by 1.8. For a dollar*, he says, *you get 1.475 marks. Of course you pay a commission for the transaction and the equivalents change every day.* All this he tells me, who has to add six and five on my fingers.

Several hours later, after we stand in the aisle for a while, after the movie, I have my hand across Jack's lap. He sleeps and I withdraw my hand and let him go into his own world free-falling into dreams without me following, for a while anyway.

After a short peace with angels, it's 1:15 A.M. by Minnie's gloved hands, and we're over Ireland. It's morning and break-fast comes down the aisle. *If you set your watch ahead seven hours, the shift will seem easier,* he says. *Don't go by the time you left.*

There are a few ice crystals on the window in the early dawn. Over the English Channel, the ground speed is 506 miles an hour. The outside temp is minus seventy-four degrees Fahrenheit. Altitude thirty-seven thousand feet.

I am slow to adapt. I'm slow to apprehend that's France down there. There are small fields with borders. It's not America under me, but a place I've never seen. There aren't as many roads and something is different. I can't quite define it. Except maybe when you take an old wool jacket out of the downstairs closet, and it doesn't fit.

It's the middle of the night in my backyard and, nearing Zurich, there are little moons jumping across the glass—something like a row of marigolds. It's an illusion of some sort, like you wish your old marriage was. You're daydreaming an out-of-sync memory, and suddenly the wheels go down to meet the earth as a man might realize he's falling.

At least time's not divided, then multiplied by 1.6. There's a simple seven-hour difference.

### 5/20 Zurich–Basel–Freiburg

It's 11:55 A.M. in Zurich. 4:55 A.M. in my backyard, though I don't tell Jack as we sit in the airport. I feel amazingly awake after two hours of sleep. *It will hit you,* he says in the airport, *like a marathon runner hits the wall.*

From Zurich, there's a bright, clean twenty-minute flight to Basel.

A large, new black Audi takes us from Basel to Freiburg. The driver doesn't speak English and the autobahn goes by at ninety in the shade.

We arrive in Freiburg at 1:30 P.M. At my house in St. Paul, it's 6:30 A.M. *Will you stop that,* he says. But I've lost seven hours somewhere, and I want them back.

We eat in the open with other writers from the conference, walk around the square, and at the Hotel Rothhaus, Jack and I sleep for a few hours. When we wake around seven in the evening, we make love, God forgive us, when the bells ring on Martinskirche across the square. There are always bells ringing in Freiburg, though later I find they're sometimes the bells at the town hall where people gather to get married in the mornings.

I look into my one suitcase for what I brought, trying to get by with as little as possible because I have to pull it over Germany for the next two weeks. Not wanting to be burdened with luggage in train stations always up or down long stairways, not wanting to get tired of the same two linen skirts and white blouses.

We try to sleep again, but I'm awake in the night. After all, it's midafternoon at my house and I think of my cat sunning herself in the yard. I listen to Jack sleep and wake, and we both drift like a flutter of pigeons over the square.

Finally I hit sound sleep and it's ten in the morning when the maid opens the door. The shutters close out all the light and some of the sound from the street below. We missed breakfast and wander in the street disoriented, looking for rolls and coffee.

I'm still struggling to be here. I sit on the square by the fountain and watch the people. I sit vacantly listening to water run in the *bachle*, the narrow water trough at the edge of the cobblestone street. Somewhere the angels play a cello and a violin.

5/21–5/24 The four-day conference in Freiburg

Readings and panels. There are many of us there. The audience asks: What makes America work? Do I have a gun? How does America like not being first? Though I think we are. How many people are trying to move to Japan?

The writers on the panel are from different mainstream and minority groups in America: Two African Americans. Two Native Americans. Several Anglos. A naturalized American born in India. We disagree. It's really what they want to hear. America's not just one country anymore. It sounds like many. There's even a difference between those in the same group. I talk about it when I sit next to a man who reads how he is from the elk people.

*But America's a mess,* one young man says from the back of the room, and his friends laugh. Later, when I talk to him, he says if he could live anywhere, it would be Portland, Oregon.

One afternoon during the conference, after a lunch in the country on new white asparagus, we get on a bus for a ride through the Black Forest. In the mid-eighteenth century, some of my mother's people came from this area—I brought the first page of her genealogy. Three brothers named Siceloff, and their sister, came from Strasbourg when it was Germany. They also came from Kandel and Minfield. One of the brothers and his family were killed by Indians near Schuylkill County, Pennsylvania on their way to North Carolina.

On the bus as we leave Freiburg, a sign reads *Kandel*. I think no, we can't be going there. It's too much of a coincidence. We take the road up the mountain in the large bus climbing higher than a window washer reaching the glass of heaven. Wiping the bright sun—there's some kind of large black speck on the window. I try to pick it with my fingers. But it's someone in a hang glider soaring above us. Then another. Everyone comments. At the top of the mountain, we see the ramp where you can put on your wings and run to the sky, without fear of falling. And there on top of the mountain, the word *Kandel*. I pick up a rock from the place that could have been the origin of part of my heritage. My first time in Europe—and I come to it?

Later, back in Freiburg, in Strossberg Park above Freiburg, the day before we leave, I listen to the birds, the church bells, a few people talking in their houses. There are flowers, the smell of blossoms, the buzz of a fly. There's some sort of peace that I like.

## 5/25 Regensburg

Our first Eurail trip. I can't pull or push the compartment door when we get on the train. *It slides, dear,* Jack tells me. Soon Germany rushes by again. This time at a slower pace. I see the steep vineyards from the train. Even the hills have to work here. We pass red-roofed villages. Stacks of wood by the houses. A river. A Fiat factory. Small fields of wheat, corn, potatoes. Fruit trees. Poppies and irises. On a bridge in Offenburg, a mother holds her child waving at the train.

We transfer at Karlsruhe. Tug our heavy bags down the stairs then up to another track. The conductor tells me to get my feet off the seat in the small compartment as I rest. At Vaihingen, there's another stop, and another at Stuttgart. In Ansbach, I want to remember the lilacs.

In Regensburg, I give a talk at the university.

## 5/26–5/27 Nuremberg

I talk at the University in Nuremberg, and am paid. The man at the German-American House and Jack sit in his office and tell me all the money I'll be making. Behind them on the wall, a historical poster calling emigrants to America. Fields and oxen and plows. Maybe land was what brought my mother's ancestors from Germany to America.

But what the man from the German-American House doesn't say is that, after the Freiburg conference, I'm responsible for room and board, which is expensive in Germany. Soon I find that half my money goes for the room alone. So now it's mostly my money we're traveling on. Later, I find the embassy in Bonn has even wired some of it to the hotel in Regensburg and charged me for the wire. I feel a sense of betrayal. It seems to me the story men have always told. And I don't buy it anymore. I'm mad at Jack as we stand outside the museum. Not only do I not make much, but I have to swallow the story that I do, and I'm supposed to act happy about it. I say cruel words. I tell him what I think. I call him *gigolo*.

And the real problem is that there are five days we're on our own because of a religious or national holiday. They really can't tell us what it is. Whitsuntide. When, well—something happened. Not the ascension of Christ. Not Pentecost. Maybe the assumption of Mary. No. Someone else. No one can put it in English. Finally someone says *It's Father's Day when the fathers go out and get drunk.* Whatever it is, everything is closed from Thursday to Sunday.

We stand in front of the Germanisches National Museum, *Das grösste Museum deutscher Kunst und Kultur,* arguing—the loud Americans. Then we swallow our anger and go in. Both of us are wounded. We walk through the Middle Ages past the horse armor, halberds, cannons, crossbows, helmets, battle axes, swords—the map of a war encampment: *Die song Schlacht im Walde zevischen der Reichsstadt Nurmberg vad dem Markgrafen Katimer von Brandenberg das 19 June 1502.*

Yes, that's the world—full of spears, faceplates, iron stars.

*Why do you doubt the war in the heart of man?* I ask, to open up another area of disagreement between us. *We have both good and bad in us. It's the same now as it was then.* I tell him. *Look at this museum—War and Church.*

We have wounded one another and now we're going to struggle to find the power to forgive. That's what determines a relationship. But not yet. He is going to speak his anger. I get ready for the fall away from him back to myself—

He tells me how I wanted to hurt him. Deliberately. It's more than a general anger at men. *I uncovered you,* he said, *you're sensual, and what's more, you're mean-spirited.* He delivers his attack.

I feel guilty of everything—and am. Why does he think I go to church? *I'm selfish,* is why. Christ was nailed to the cross so I could face the darkness in my heart. So I could look up past the angels and archangels straight through that darkness into light.

I think of my companion in terms of indecision and slowness. His suppression of my passion. But maybe it needs suppressing. I have the memory of my own war. When I held myself with my arms and was alone. I risked knocking down and rebuilding. I risk something every time I tell him how I feel. But there's going to be communication this time.

We see more of Nuremberg. The parts of the city rebuilt after war. New brick and old. The smell of car exhaust in heavy midday traffic. The courtroom of the trial.

I feel like an intruder. I feel overwhelmed. I was a child in another country, but I was alive during the hearings in this large, hollow, wood-paneled courtroom where men tried to establish some kind of rules—some kind of rational standards by which we could determine boundaries of behavior. We had to define the violations. Say these war crimes are inhumane. We cannot ever go beyond these boundaries again. If we want to remain human beings.

The sun flicked through the trees and spotted the heavy walls and oversized marble moldings of the doors. I wanted to leave. I wanted to think about something else. I felt like I had been walking a long way with shoes on the wrong feet. I was afraid that a courtroom was inadequate to contain the enormity of what happened.

Die Tauben

There are pigeons in the square in Nuremberg. They eat off the cobblestones. The one I see trying to hold his foot up, sometimes squatting on the cobblestones. For all I know they are angels and mostly they are pushed or kicked out of the way. They could wish instead to be animals on a walk. See the dogs here and there. Or pieces of language still on the leash of the tongue. A few of the pigeons are brown. But mostly they are gray with greenish or lilac necks, as though they'd rubbed against a fish and caught the iridescent wetness. Their heads bob. Their red feet waddle. Their red eyes look for something to eat. Even the wounded one. They carry a gentle power. Not of this earth, but some lovely invigoration like pondweeds moving back and forth. Or someone's hand carefully cleaning a window.

## 5/28–6/1 Würzburg—Heidelberg

On the train again, the towns start going by. Darmstadt. Bensheim. Then for a night Würzburg where Jack visits a friend at the university, and on to Heidelberg.

The fall into war is here. Some planes unloaded their cargo of bombs in the country just to make a dump. Others hit their mark. The patched and mismatched church windows tell of it.

The next morning, Jack has to leave for America at 6:45. The wake-up call didn't come, but he's up anyway, the way you are sometimes with something on your mind.

The hotel boy is asleep, he guesses. Could I put on my dress? There's no phone book in the room and he wants me to go downstairs and call a taxi. He's thinking of making it to the train station in Heidelberg—to the airport in Frankfurt. He's already on his way to Zurich to Chicago to Minneapolis. Leaving me in a country whose language I don't speak with a whole Sunday to pass by myself.

I go to the lobby and find the phone number for a cab and my companion leaves.

In the breakfast room of the hotel, a woman paces like a hen waiting for breakfast. I hate these little breakfast rooms crowded with tables. No one talks. Just clinks their silverware. Only one little lidded pitcher of coffee. No more. Everything as if still rationed. As if still hearing the planes overhead.

It's hard to open the coffee. My hand hurts. Maybe the heat of the coffee pulled it on harder. *Rotpunkt*. The name of the pot. I'm tired of a place where everything is strange.

I spend two hours reading a diary someone left in a drawer in my room. I clean up. Sit at the window. I'm on my own. I walk up the cobblestone street of old Heidelberg. I'm ready to move on. To follow him back to America. That afternoon, I walk again. I sit on a park bench for a while. The pigeons feed nearby.

Sunday evening, there's a concert of organ, drum, and three xylophones. People gather in the front pews. A woman with her beautiful bones. The students frumped in jeans and T-shirts from the world's markets. And there, in the corner, the stained glass window of August 6, 1945, commemorating the A-bomb. It's the reminder of another atrocity. But it was outside Germany. Though connected. Our red globe broken open. Spilling its lava. It marks our arrival at the West Pole. The postatomic age. I listen to the concert in the church rebuilt after World War II. The xylophones like icicles. The drum tap-dancing. The gong of the wild organ. I hear the zootie, discordant sound of our fall into the atomic age. Its hoot over a molten core.

At noon the next day, I give a talk on Native American literature and answer questions.

Why America works is how it handles its diversity and problems. Saying what I think. How we are a complexity of selfishness and selflessness. A complicated, compliant nation of working conflicts.

Everywhere, I see the Japanese. The piece of cauliflower on my plate at supper looks like a small atomic cloud.

6/2–6/4 Frankfurt—Trier

I take the train to Frankfurt. In Frankfurt, I give a talk. Then on to Trier the next day, where I read my poems at the university.

Afterwards, I only want to go back to America. I think of gravity with its hands always on us. I could be sitting on a park bench in Heidelberg by myself. Thinking of war. I could be washing a window nearly reaching heaven. Hearing angels in the flush of pigeon wings—their flight swift as the slip of a man who is suddenly reminded we don't have wings.

# The Woman Who Became a Bear

Imagine coming over a pass and seeing the mountains go on and on. You get used to the earth the way it is in the Midwest. Then suddenly it's different. You're bowled over by the change. The abrupt jarring of what it means.

I'd been in Tucson for two months with my companion. My partner, friend. He had a sabbatical, and I did. Now we were on the way back to Minnesota. The car packed so full I couldn't see out the back. Just the rearview mirrors on each side. A little pallet in the back seat between the hanging clothes for my cat.

We're traveling north on Highway 77 from Tucson to Interstate 44 at Holbrook.

I'd gotten used to the desert. There were mountains there too. Five of them surrounding Tucson. Santa Catalina, Rincon, Santa Rita, Tucson, Tortolita. I'd see them, but they were part of the landscape from my front door. Now in the distance there was a range of mountains, and north of them, even more.

I'm driving. It's my car. We're sharing expenses. The car and gas are mine. Housing is his because I refused to pay part of the rent. We each take care of our meals. He makes nearly twice what I do. Has his house paid for. While a third of my salary goes for my mortgage. But you see *we're equals,* he says. Get it? That means he doesn't pay for me. Though to be fair, he does pay more. Because I also refused to pay part of the utilities in Tucson. And once in a while he buys my dinner.

I watch the names along Highway 7. Corizzo Creek. Cottonwood Wash. Four Mile Draw. Washboard Wash.

As we drive down into the Salt River Canyon, I tell him it reminds me of the Grand Canyon, except you can't drive into it.

At the bottom we stop at the Salt River. It's at Beckers Butte, when we start back up, that I see the caves high in the cliffs of the mountains.

It's March just before the heat sets in. The season when thunder wakes. The season I guess when bears come out of hibernation. Though I don't know much about bears, except I've come out of a cave also.

I'm beginning to hear my own voice. I talk and sometimes there's this sound. Is that what it's like? Climbing the mountain road from Salt River with my car loaded to the ears.

I like this one voice growling in me.

I don't know what made the caves high in the walls of Beckers Butte. Maybe wind or the birds pecked them out.

There are places that need stories. Places that would not *be* without them. Sometimes they call for your story and you don't want to give it. Expose yourself and the little hangnail of your humanity.

I feel another growl in my throat. He can't hear. The noise of the car. The wind. I growl again. It comes from a will of my own and doing what I want, even if at times I'm not always sure what I'm doing.

The winds are strong on the road. You pass a truck with a blue tarp over it floppy as the sky you see moving overhead. Large flat-bottomed clouds over the earth. You know it also. Maybe that's the uneven way the earth looks upside down to the clouds.

I think it's what angers me about my earlier life. I was a housewife for nearly twenty years. When I divorced I left without anything. I didn't get paid. But my companion, my friend, has always worked. I raised my children and tended to family matters. While he's had nearly thirty years of accrual. But I gave to my children. Like the bear who feeds her young while she herself doesn't eat.

Afterwards, an idea planted itself like a governing constitution in my head. My giving is over except what I want to give, and nothing will interfere with my life again.

I pass the road construction where they were losing a part of the road down the steep canyon.

I pass redbuds and greasewood of Navajo country. Their culture of harmony. I drive away from it getting my car out of alignment. My nose out of joint.

It only takes a few hours and you're back on the flat land. Like a journey over eight thousand feet, you climb and descend slowly in your car packed with your books and papers and word processor and household goods for two months.

We left Minnesota for Tucson on January 21. I had to slide the boxes to my car down the back walk because it was covered with ice. I squatted behind the boxes to slide down the walk also. Then we drove through sleet and rain until Kansas. In Amarillo I washed my car of its several hundred miles of dried road slush.

Later, I will have to have my wheels aligned. Two tires replaced. My steering wheel will wobble when I brake.

My companion is nine years older than I am. When we argue, I wish I had his accumulation of salary and benefits. He wishes he had my years.

It's also his lack of direction in our relationship I think about. I have to know where I'm going. I think how maybe children do that. You can't plan but stay stationary for them. Until they're grown. Then you can take off with your own life again. Maybe that's why I want to drive while he rides. He's secure. I'm still traveling.

There's a Chippewa word that means traveling woman. *Equaysayway*. I'm not Chippewa. I'm part Cherokee, part white. A combination of possibilities. A whole of movable parts. Maybe inconsistent. But I'm going.

I could even drive off on my own.

It's what they get. Part of my father's lesson was that I could work and earn my keep. Or part of it anyway, in the beginning. Then I would not cost him as much.

I could make it without my companion. After I got past the hard wall of being alone again. I remember my first Christmas break at Macalester College when I moved to Minnesota. Riding the bus to my aunt's house in Kansas City and back. I only wanted to stay there a few days. Then I had almost two weeks without anyone to talk to but my cat.

But what did I get with my independence? I guess I earned a place on the bench. A seat behind the wheel. It was what my mother who was born in 1909 and married in 1933 never knew. But I still feel I lost a lot. My companion now gets my love without responsibility. It seems that men still come out ahead.

Maybe I can stop whining. I have an occupation now. I can make other noises in the night. I already do. I'm quite aware of it. Bear noises.

Can you believe it?—what is most important to me now is my work.

You can imagine coming over the pass—

# This Is for You

I think of you showing up in my life like a delivery arrived a day late. Just when I thought it was over. You turned in my drive. You presented yourself well. Took the first freight elevator you found. Didn't ask directions. Went down into my heart. I can feel you shifting boxes. Moving baggage. I can feel you down there cleaning out.

# There's a Word for It because It Happens or Maybe It Happens because There's a Word for It

So you came to me and I knew to love you. Let God come and get me now that I'm in your arms. Let these words be a shield against the ordinary days that consumed me worse than God. Let me know the terror of your dark. Let me hold you and ask never to give back my love. On this word shield I draw for you. You bring desire. This could be my church. Your arms around me. If I were something wild and you came like a sail. The way wind blows across rabbit fur and lifts the little rows of waves. Then you would have been this white tablet. This pencil moving with breakers of waves migrating into shore. Saying this is my worship. This is my new world. I know in church there's a place where love is. I've felt it before. Heavenly and not mine but God and Christ and the angels and something I can't really belong to. At least now. But if this new world goes with the next traffic light well for a moment your car stopped here. In my garage and I get up earlier than you and sit at the table on Sunday and have another gift. The blue anemone you brought with others in a vase. And I hear the scratch of this pencil on paper writing words called *gift* because they say something of love. They're all we've got to tell us we are found.

# WRITING, LANGUAGE, AND STORIES

# Comment

*Story is all we have.* According to Leslie Silko and other Native writers.

It was Kim Blaeser, an Ojibwa critic, I heard say
*We have to know our stories.*
*We have to tell our stories.*
*We have to retell our stories in our own way.*
*We have to know stories we don't know.*
*We have to know stories they make about us.*
*We have to know their stories.*

Well, there's a term I made up, *Coyosmic.* Literary theory according to Coyote. Who thinks *flocoly* is a melancholy flock of sheep (whose wool will make Navajo blankets). (Then the sheep will be content.) (For which a new word will have to be invented.)

We have to understand not by Western, but by tribal-centered criticism. Its continual de-formation. Re-formation. A moving process of saying a story. Letting it go in the act of being.

A dehegemonized setup.

What we know runs contrary to Western tradition. It violates our tradition. We must transform from within Native American literature into a *bicult.* Not giving them ours in their own way. Which is what they want.

We need a code-switching, mixed-blood metaphor. A buffalo convoy conveying the interpreted transport.

Our own territory moved-over unthreading. For the sweat-lodge-hot rock of human thought. A dispossession and repo of the nothing we've shared in the possession at the wide mouth of meaning.

The little blasting cap of the word.

We have to give sound to the sacred wilderness of the silenced landscape. These words in the process of becoming.

I want language to stomp dance the dry ground of my heart.

That's literary theory in the cosmos of Coyote.

Who is meaning and no meaning.

Variegated with the fragments of each.

A series of crossings.

A movement of broken fragments.

Coyote presents from what he takes from each.

I heard Jerry Rudquist, Macalester College art professor, say his paintings are *containers of connections*.

In large, you have to tell a story with reused and interconnecting tools. It's not an act in itself, but storying for generating the-sake-of-story-making-its-fragments-for.

What would be an Indian aesthetic? A Coyote's critical theory? The latest writing that came late. The stories just beginning to be *wrote*.

# Speaking the Corn into Being

There was a time when what you said actually happened. If you needed to hunt, you spoke the herd into the woods or prairie. You spoke your arrow into the animal. You gave thanks to the Great Spirit for the reciprocal process of word and "happening." You gave thanks to the animal for its life. It was a time when the word was ceremony. Not so much a chronological time such as "long ago," but a conditional sense of the word pushed through to Word.

Speech had the power to become physical property. Maybe still does. Nobody knew how it happened, but that's the way it was. It seemed to be connected with oral tradition. When there were no books or written laws or any way to write them. When everything was carried in the belief system of the tribe and was a matter of the heart and head. When this word/object relationship was intact.

The word also could be transferred at times just by thinking. Without sound. In fact it's not really the words but the thought, the spirit or energy behind what is said. Putting into being the vital life-force of which words are only the carriers.

We've lost those times. They hardly exist in memory even among the old ones. Ask Cherokees on the streets of Tahlequah, Oklahoma, about the meaning of their language and they'd probably say "What?" They talk about the things people talk about. They might say that "words making things" sounds like the ancestors talking. They'd probably say "Go away."

But somehow there's still the sense of the word as a creative force. The power of the word is to be respected. Words are a tribe with different "duties." There's the word as sacred, as holy, as ceremony. There are ordinary words of conversation. There's silence, which is a powerful internal structure. Even the land has a voice. And the animals. Once they spoke too, but gave up their language. According to legend, they didn't want to be like us.

My concept of the word, the spoken word, is an image I have. It goes back to the time before we killed the word. Before we put it in its little coffin which the written form is. When the word was alive. When it was spirit. When what we spoke coordinated conditions (brought into harmony arrow and animal). Or what we spoke actually served as a causal function. Words as transformers. As makers of things that happened.

I want to remember what it was like. Those times before the alphabet aren't here anymore, but neither are they gone. They wake now and then at moments when something stirs them. Or when, for an instant, I catch a peripheral glance of something that must have been like them. Though I have changed from what the ancestors were, and language and the world in which that language operated have changed as well. And in the end, what does it matter? That way of life, despite all its power, was defeated.

Now this is the Cherokee understanding of the spoken word, the voice, anyway. In our tradition, people do not simply speak about the world, they speak the world into being. What we say is intricately intertwined with what we are and can be. To the Cherokee people, all things in the world have a voice— and that voice carries life. Storying gives shape to meaning. This concept of speech and voice is based on a notion that the voice does not speak alone, but generations of voices speak. They must be heard and understood by others and added onto by them. When we speak we take the power of the spoken word and infuse it with new breath. We add our voice to story so it shifts, changes, renews with the multiplicity of meanings and the variables of possibilities. To keep words alive and elastic. To keep them the shape-changers they have to be for our survival.

The voice and the thought that rides upon the voice are the challenge. What you speak is spoken into an energy field or field of force that has consequence. The breath forming words is holy. The sound and shape of them breathed into being.

The Cherokee knew their words had the power to create. That's also the guardian, the check and balance, of the word. Its power to generate force. What you said could last for generations. Therefore you guarded your words. You made them count in the oral tradition. You spoke them responsibly. You kept in mind that what the speaker says affects the speaker as much as the spoken to.

Now this is what I have to say about speaking the corn into being.

In the old days the farmers did not know the day of planting. It was announced by the holy men. Then the orators would come and sing the seed corn into the field and the field into the form from which the corn would rise in the process of the seeds breaking. Then someone, usually the grandmother, would sit on her platform speaking the crows away from the seeded fields until the seeds were established in stalks and corn tassels waving and the corn itself could speak the crows away. The corn was mixed with words all summer. The fields were never without sound. Even after harvest, a green-corn ceremony honored the new crop. During the storing process. Even during baking or cooking, a woman would speak to the corn. Tell it stories.

There was an interconnectedness of things.

*And it shall come to pass in that day, I will hear, saith the Lord, I will hear the heavens, and they shall hear the earth; And the earth shall hear the corn . . . and [the corn] shall hear [the people]. Hosea 2:21-22*

Some of the Cherokee were evangelized by Christian missionaries. They found similarities in Yahweh and the Great Spirit because the Judeo-Christian God also spoke the world into being. He had the power to join mind and word. He knew the wholeness of being. In fact, there are stories that the Great Spirit made us because he wanted to share that power. He mixed us with the dust of the ground and his breath. It's breath that gives us kinship with the Great Spirit. Breath is in the sacredness of the spoken word. In turn, we are creators when we speak.

We are accountable for our words.

But the spirit of the word is smothered under papers and documents and files and debates and laws and libraries and books. There also should be a category for ignorance and indifference. Just as denominations smother the spirit of the Great Spirit. I'm not against the new world. But it gave up a lot. Mainly without knowing what it lost.

Sometimes I speak my *corn* into being. I speak to my words. I say to them, you will talk in the old way. My son is a teacher, my daughter an attorney. I say to them, your words will speak your path into being.

But the Cherokee lost their way of life in the coming of the new. Yet in the stillness sometimes I see a word come to life.

It's an ancient power.

This is what I have to say.

Over a spring break I made another trip for the United States Information Agency, to a country where there was no freedom of expression. What a person was to believe was broadcast into the streets over loudspeakers several times a day. There were armed soldiers at checkpoints. That's what you have to do to guard against a politically and morally fractured, pluralistic society, which the United States is. Full of diversity and discord and messiness and life.

Besides, where do you stop regulating once you begin?

In the old way of speaking, the speaker always remembers he connects not only to others (this includes the unseen past and future generations who surround him), but also to the original creator of speech himself, the Great Spirit, from whom this process was given and learned. I'm not looking back and saying that then was good and now is bad. That's not true at all.

Things aren't as simple as absolutes.

There is never a lone voice that can be judged true or false. The voice always connects to the something it speaks into being, and brings with it not only the thought or spirit of the speaker but also the accumulated voices that ride upon any single voice, and, in turn, that something-brought-into-being affects other voices that speak with others and so forth. Without the polarity of truth and falsity. Without that concept. In fact, the same words can be both "good" and "bad" depending on the circumstance and the speaker. An "alive" word can travel both ways at once.

Language should be a ceremony changing the way we think. It operates in conditions that allow it to operate. Language doesn't work with a harness. It has to move with the changing sameness it always has. The same changeableness. Those subtle differences or inferences that change the context. That shift the meaning of the text. So that we are renewed and not tied to circumstance. Meaning with changeable consistency. We have to reflect it in our words. And in turn we are reflected.

Language has a holy-clown element that goes backward or contrariwise. To give possibilities. To lose the bonds. So the tribe isn't stuck with hunger. Or unalterable, negative situations. Yes, that's something like it.

Because all sorts of words set all sorts of energy fields into being, our words light a match to the dark, and the dark has a substance. Or if not, then darkness is a void that becomes something according to our words.

And you see in the end we're going to talk in circles which the true migration path is. So that the process of the journey is more important than the arrival point. Inconclusiveness and open-endedness are also a part of Native thought. Which irritates the Western mind. But it's been around a long time. It just hasn't been recognized by the present dominant culture. Many voices, many points of view, full of contradictions and moving variables and kinetic energies which keep a civilization breathing its life breath. Take away a language and all its possibilities and you extinguish a people, or at least the spirit of a people.

Because meaning has to be multiplaced as it speaks, which reflects the multiplacement of the Great Spirit and his relationship to otherness.

Our language, and ourselves for that matter, are basically spiritual according to Cherokee belief. The world-that-is doesn't usually consider that to be a point. So maybe it will also miss the Cherokee concept of words.

The nature of meaning is moving. Words changing in combination with other words. Kinetic beings rolling around like marbles. It's in our voice. Our nation. Which is language.

I would like to hear the Cherokee grandfathers with their long-stemmed pipes and turbans sitting around the brusharbor talking about these matters. Speaking the corn into being. Speaking the corn beings.

There are some stories that take seven days to tell. There are other stories that take you all your life.

# The Woman Who Made Eyes

> "They have animals called Medicine Dogs
> that stand high as an elk but have no antlers."
> "But do they bark and warn the camp when strangers
> approach?"
>
> "Antelope and the Engineers"
> R. David Edwards in *American Indian Identity*

I think writing is a matter of seeing too. Of making from inner vision. Of intention. Purpose. Meaning.

Bringing into being.

I think the magic of speech also happens in writing.

I want to see imagination in writing. The ordinary and extraordinary combined. There's an import store on Grand Avenue in St. Paul that carries what I want in my writing. Sometimes I walk past and see the wooden animals imported from Mexico in the windows. A hot pink hyena, a fuchsia doghorse, an anteater with a beaver tail, the ducks with rabbit ears. Writing is supposed to make things happen like that. New alliances should be formed.

On a recent trip, I met a woman who made eyes. Her job was in prosthetics, and she had a book of people's faces she had changed. Some who had had wandering or dead or missing eyes. She made them look like they should.

Imagination in writing is not only entering the freakish or unbelievable, but more often shaking the ordinary ground. But learning also is the shaking of boundaries. It's moving fences. The thermos of the sky above them.

Writing should break the rules for the sake of discovering or creating new inventions, new followings, new horses that also bark.

To see the white-flowered head of the yucca as a bride's veil or a Hopi dancer. Or to see glass antlers when rain freezes on the branches of the backyard tree. Or to see sundown in the head of the red-eared slider turtle.

I think we have to continue Adam's work of naming. Only we have more than animals. We can name the whole earth. And all of our experience on it. It's our job to be responders and leave the earth a little less inarticulate. We're the ones who make it meaningful.

Giving words to earth.

What else do I have but language?

I think wisdom is to look at things in their own light. Not premeditated by interior modes of landscape. Or entanglements with self. But how about the artist who has to have subjectivity? Creativity is the opposite of objectivity. To see through the filter of. To soak through one's sight.

And how to do both.

That's what we need. A horse that barks to warn against attack.

A woman who makes eyes.

# The Story

*Once a woman tried to run from a man who chased her. When he got near and she knew he would catch her, she turned into a tree. The man chopped down the tree and built a cabin from it. In the night he could hear her moan. Finally she talked the wind into kicking a spark from the fireplace and the cabin burned to the ground.*

It's what we have left of *story*. The fragments. But we build from what we have left. It's a starting point. A chase.

And once I think I have it, it changes form. I can still think I capture the whole of what I purpose in writing. Yes. But it's only in the process of reshaping.

Sometimes in a story I think I hear an old voice. I try to nail it, but the voice calls to the wind to change it. And I have nothing but a few moans.

But I build a book. You see. If I have the pages around me like walls. And even if a spark burns it to the ground. Yes. Maybe there's *the story*. The trail of smoke from something that was.

Writing is a voice calling to the wind. A few moans in the walls of the pages. Maybe it's the oral voice in the written word. The writer chasing it. Well. You could say you hear your story the way you hear someone call out from sleep. If you wake them. You destroy what you captured. But you would have at least a residue. If you get to it fast enough.

# A Short Story Is Something Happening

My first story forinstance was about riding a bus.
The driver's name was *Homer*.
You know the plaque for his name inside the door.
Now after my transformative years.
Say thirty of them. Roughly.
I write about driving the bus myself.
I may even be the bus.

Or I am the road.
More than that. I am the relationship between
the bus the road and the land.
Not any one object but the living process of movement
through time and space.

No one text dominating but all of them relating and
interacting and
you know
the examined life.

But the first story I wrote.

• • •

It's really not important. What I'm going to tell you. It happened
a long time ago. I still remember but I don't think about it much
anymore. I mean you just can't sit around thinking about something that happened a long time ago. It just happened. I don't care
anymore. But I guess I'll tell you about it.

You know how some people have things they really like, like
going to the opera or watching a show. Things like that never
meant anything to me. I watch trucks. The big ones. The diesels

*branded with their name. Eighteen wheelers. I watch them on the highway. There's nothing wrong with that. If I were a nine-year-old boy on my bicycle. But I'm not. I'm a girl. And I'm twenty. But I was eighteen when it happened. It was a long time ago.*

• • •

When I read a story
I want to know who the story is happening to
and where I am.
I want to see the setting.
I want to hear the voice of the narrator.
And I want to hear real people talking words I recognize
as real words.
I want to connect with immediacy with what's happening.
I don't want to have to stop and ask what's going on here.

• • •

*I have never ridden in a truck. The closest I came was the time I rode the bus back to school. That's what I want to tell you about. I was a freshman at the University of Missouri then. I was going back after a weekend at my house in Kansas City. My brother took me to the station. It was the first time I had been in a place like that. Not actually the first. I had been there when I was a kid. But this was really the first time. I mean what do you know when you're a kid? A kid can be in the crummiest bus station and it will seem like Fairy Land Park. Anyway I walked into the building. I think I saw every kind of people that ever was. I sat in one of the long rows of wooden benches with my suitcases while my brother bought my ticket. There was a long line. I had to wait so I just sat there and looked around. An old man in clothes that didn't fit sat sleeping across from me. And sailors and girls that looked like Kewpie dolls. And fat mothers with bunches of little kids trying to keep them corralled. I read all the signs. "No spitting on the floor" and ones like that. I really don't think you'd care to hear about it.*

*Finally I heard over the loudspeaker that the bus was at Gate 3. My brother picked up my suitcases and we went to the door. A bus ride. I thought it would be like riding in a truck. I got on the bus and sat in the second seat. The first seats were taken. There was an old lady by the window. I asked her if I could sit there. I couldn't decide if she said yes or no so I just sat down. She sat there looking straight ahead at the "Step down to aisle" sign on the back of the front seat.*

*The driver got on. He wasn't like I thought he'd be. He pulled a little plaque of metal out of his shirt pocket and put it between "Your Operator" and "Safe, Reliable, Courteous." It said "Homer Collins." Homer Collins for Christ's sake. What a name. He wasn't like the truck drivers but what can you expect on a bus?*

• • •

But most of all. When I read a short story.
The conflict.
As close as the first words of the story
should be the conflict.
That's the way the story is.
So the conflict in my story is this girl who talks like she's been in bus stations all her life. But really hasn't. Why the difference between the apparent and the real? Between her manner and the actual facts of her life? This toughness she assumes yet hasn't really proved to have. Is the conflict within herself? Maybe her parents don't value her. Not openly of course. But there's always something in their treatment of her that says you're not really what we wanted in a daughter. Your unattractiveness is a detriment to our family. In fact we didn't want a daughter at all. Unless she was beautiful and intelligent.

And what's the relationship between the narrator and her brother? And why trucks? If something is introduced with the power to transport the story into going someplace. Into destination. Then it had better be used. So where is the bus taking this punkish girl? Not only to Columbia, Missouri, certainly, but to what change in her character, which will be consistent with what she already is.

Now the movement of events through time.
The plot and action.
What happens to lead the reader through the story
and the order of the leading.

• • •

*I saw my brother walk across the street to the car. He turned around and looked at the bus. But he couldn't see me because of the dark windows. I've seen Greyhound buses before. You can't see in the windows. You know the people are in there but you can't see them.*

*Then Homer Collins started the bus. I didn't see how he did it because I was watching my brother drive away. The first thing I noticed was the way the bus shook. I could feel it in my cheeks. A sack that the old lady had on her lap fell between us. I handed it back to her and she said something else that I couldn't understand. We started backing up, past the other buses. There were several big jerks and then we started forward. We turned right out of the bus station because it was a one-way street. It was the only way we could go. Then we turned right at the next corner and at the next and headed west to the highway.*

• • •

Maybe she feels the world has ignored her. She doesn't even tell us her name. And doesn't she know anyone to ride with back to the university? What is not being said?

• • •

*At Eighteenth Street men were drilling into the curb. There was a bump in the road that rocked the bus like a giant cradle. The old lady next to me didn't notice. She didn't seem to notice anything. Then we were downtown and I leaned over to look up at the build- ings. The tinted windows made everything look better.*

• • •

The narrator talks about counting streets and passing billboards and houses and vacant lots. Then she finds she can look straight at the low sun through the tinted windows.

• • •

*The old lady must have thought I was looking at her because she turned real quick and looked straight at me. Finally we were on bypass 40. I looked at the old lady to see if she noticed that we were almost to the highway but she didn't. She was looking at the "Step down to aisle" sign again. I wanted to look out the window but I didn't. I could see through the front windshield there were big open fields and we were missing them. Then we came to an all-night restaurant and I knew we were at the junction before I saw the sign. It said Interstate 70 with an arrow pointing straight up. We stopped at the red light. Homer Collins must have been looking around too. The bus stopped with a big jerk. Then when he pulled ahead to turn onto Highway 70 the bus jumped over the curb. I was beginning to think that old Homer hadn't driven too many buses.*

• • •

Then they're on the highway. Another bus passes and the drivers wave and the narrator thinks this is what it must be like in trucks. The bus moves through the little towns in Missouri. The old lady gets off in Danby. The girl moves over to the window and a man gets on. She watches the old lady walking toward someone in a parked car under a tree with her sack and her shopping bag.

• • •

*"Is this seat taken?"*
*"No."*
*"May I sit here?"*
*"Yeah."*
*The bus started up again. I looked out the window for a long time then decided to read more of the* Iliad. *We had to read it for an English class. It was getting dark so I turned on the light above*

me. *I read for a while then and when I looked up again it had started to rain. But I didn't realize it for a while. I guess I didn't know it was raining until I saw it on the windshield. The noise was there but I guess I hadn't heard it. Anyway I was trying to read the* Iliad *with the bus rocking and the rain and Homer, and Ulysses, I guessed, next to me.*

*The last I remember was the sun was there. I looked again and it was gone.*

. . .

Maybe it's time to experiment.
To invent the text itself.
Maybe the girl's journey on some dark road under the
moon. Or maybe some New Iliad.

But that doesn't seem to work here.
I think she stays on the bus and faces reality.
The ride to Columbia, Missouri. The college she doesn't
feel a part of. The book she hasn't finished. The
isolation and loneliness of her life.

There is the usual way. The structure of conflict.
The crisis / some kind of a resolution / then further
conflict / a final climax of the crisis / then denouement
or resolution / from which something is realized / which
is the epiphany.
Something I didn't know before
that stories are supposed to have.
Something in the human condition I didn't realize
or something I see the character learn.
Or both.

Say the guy next to her is drinking whiskey out of a bottle in a sack. He smokes though a sign says not to. Homer Collins doesn't do anything about it. The man tries to talk to the girl but she ignores him.

Finally she turns off the reading light.

• • •

*"Do you mind if I smoke?"*

*"No," I said looking at the "Smoking permitted in the rear seats only" sign.*

*"Do you care for one?"*

*"No thank you."*

*"Where are you going?"*

*"Columbia. I go to school there." I could see the smoke coming from his mouth in the shadows.*

*The bus slowed down and I saw a car in front of us. A little kid was standing in the backseat looking at the bus. I guess he was scared because he had a funny look on his face. Buses follow a car so close. Then we passed.*

*"Would you care for a drink?"*

*"No." He was drinking enough for both of us. Besides, I liked beer. I was waiting for Homer to turn around or say something because there was also a "No drinking" sign. You could probably smell whiskey all over the bus. I looked out the window into the dark and tried to pretend the man wasn't there. Homer sure wasn't like truck drivers.*

*"That's a pretty skirt and blouse you have on."*

*It was a sweater. The dunce. A blue lamb's-wool skirt and sweater. "Thank you," I said anyway.*

• • •

The man tells her he's a photographer and could get off the bus with her in Columbia. He makes a pass at the girl. Say he puts his hand on her knee. She jerks it away so furiously she thinks she's hurt his feelings. She wants to put her knee back but doesn't of course. He's every man in the world who doesn't have a woman to love him. Who's on the road just looking for someone to make human contact with for a brief moment so he can be revitalized and regain his trust in human companionship and she could have given that to him but instead she looked down on him just as she had the old lady who got off the bus. Just as probably her parents do to her. But does she see this? The story follows close as the bus to a car ahead of it. But after more awkward attempts at conversation, and some landscape passing somewhere in the dark, the bus arrives in Columbia and she gets off by herself without him. Thankfully. Though she has seen into the human condition. The shiftlessness. Disenfranchisement. And she knows she is one of them. But you can't throw yourself at everyone. Is the epiphany. Especially a man who drinks on a Greyhound bus and isn't going anywhere in particular.

So what is the story saying? We're in God's hands? Or the machinery's? What can we do?

Confront the scenes head-on. Don't summarize.

· · ·

Now after all the drama and symbolism and foreshadowing.
After the possibility of the story doing something with
the concept of signs, or at least the possibility of
sign as a sign that could go somewhere.
There is whoever tells the story.
The point of view.
These are a few choices.
A narrator who knows everything and tells whatever leads
the story to its end.
A narrator who knows only what's happening in one
character's head
and still leads the story to its end.
A narrator who is a character in the story who knows only
his own head
and sometimes not even that.

And theme which is the idea running through the story.
And emotion which is the reason I read.
A story should locate both the head and heart.

If short stories are to help in any way.

Then there should be details in imagery. Fast as a
frog's tongue.

These are my choices to make.
Breakinginto the solid surface.
Bindingup the fractured.

The sandy lakeshore just underwater rippled as the
afternoon clouds.
The moon looking through the venetian blinds
of those same clouds at night.

• • •

Now what's the point of my writing?
The years I lost the way but went on as though I had it?
Through faith anyway. The simple matter of going on. When
there was nowhere to go. When I was afraid enough I could
feel myself shake. It was an endless act of days. But I had some
sort of endurance. Some sort of message to go on. Though I
would pass invisible through those years. Nothing I did could
make an impact. And nothing was real. No home. No place I
really wanted to be at the end of the journey. Just the passing of
houses through my head. I think that's why my cat is afraid
when she's in the car. The whole stilled world suddenly moves
past the window. The man who stayed on the bus was probably
my husband. He would pass silently out of my life to some unknown destination. I may have been writing my own story
without realizing it. But I kept traveling with strength I had
from some unknown source. Until finally I knew the way.

# The Stories

*from Cherokee oral tradition*

America's a turtle's back
suspended at the four directions by cords
hanging from the sky
which is solid rock
you know.
When the earth grows old, the people will die and the cords
will break and the land will sink back into the water. The Indians are afraid of this.

When the animals first climbed down to the earth
there was no light
and the animals stumbled around in the darkness. Whenever
they bumped into one another they would say *What we need is
some light.*
At last they called a meeting in the dark. The woodpecker said
they had light in their other world, the one above the water,
but who could get it?

Finally there was a voice in the grass.
*Perhaps this is something I can do.*
*Who are you?* The animals asked.
*I'm the spider. Maybe I can carry some light.*
*Ho ho.* The animals laughed.
But the spider started toward the sun, spinning a thread
behind her so she could find her way back.
She took a piece of the sun and wrapped it in her web.
Then crawled back along the thread she spun, carrying a
piece of the sun's light.
That's why the spider's web spreads like the sun's rays.
To remind the animals.

So the animals set the piece of sun on a track to go every day
across the island from east to west, just overhead. But it was
too hot this way. The animals put the sun another handbreadth
higher in the air but it was still too hot. They raised it another
time, and another, until it was just under the sky. Then it was
right, and they left it.
Now every day the sun goes along under its arch, and returns
at night on the upper side to the starting point.

People came after the animals and plants. At first there was only a brother and sister until he struck her with a fish and told her to multiply so there would be others. In seven days a child was born to her and thereafter every seven days another child was born and they increased until there was danger that the earth could not hold them. Then it was decided that a woman should have only one child a year. And it has been so ever since.

The sun was a young woman who lived in the east. Her brother, the moon, lived in the west. The young woman had a lover who came in her back window each month in the dark of the moon to court her. He would come at night and leave at daylight. Although she talked to him she could not see his face. At last she decided to find out who he was. As they were sitting in the dark, she dipped her hand in the cinders of the fireplace and rubbed it on his face, saying your face is cold you must have suffered from the wind. The next night when the moon came up in the sky his face was covered with the faint spots of soot and the sister knew he was the one coming to see her. He was so ashamed that he kept as far away as he could at the other end of the sky all night. Ever since he tries to keep a long way away from the sun and when he comes near her he makes his body thin as a ribbon so he can hardly be seen.

Now there is talk of what the stars are. No one is really sure. Some say they are balls of light. Others say they are human. But most people say they are living creatures covered with luminous fur.

One night a hunting party camping in the mountains noticed how light moved along the top of a distant ridge. They watched until the light disappeared on the other side. The next night and the next, they saw the light again along the ridge and after talking, they decided to find it. In the morning they started out and when they came to the ridge they discovered two strange objects with round bodies covered with fur and from which small heads stuck out like the heads of terrapins. As the breeze played upon the fur, showers of sparks flew out. The hunters carried them back to camp, intending to take them home to their settlements. They kept them several days and noticed how every night they would grow bright, although by day they were balls of gray fur, except the wind stirred and made sparks fly out. They kept quiet and no one thought they would escape. When on the seventh night, they suddenly rose from the ground like balls of fire and were soon above the trees. Higher and higher they went while the hunters watched until at last they were only bright points of light in the dark sky and the hunters knew they were stars.

There is talk of why the stars were on earth. Some say they fell from their constellations. Others say they came with news. But the hunters tried to keep them and the stars left before they had a chance to talk. Some say the stars are still trying to tell us something. Look at them in the night sky. All the tribes with their campfires burning, speaking to us in smoke signals or the Morse code of their twinkling.

Other people say the stars dance and twirl in the sky every night. It's the solar winds that make light fly from their fur.

But most people say the stars might have stayed with us a

while. They may have come to give us understanding. But we were intent on keeping them and forgot to listen. So now we have to work. We have to figure it out ourselves. And in the end, maybe it's better than transcending easy into the great dark sphere.

# Grandmother Library

*for the Macalester College Dewitt Wallace Library*

The books stand like ancestors on the shelves.
They sing our hunting songs.
Thank them like the animals for their lives.

Float into the white clouds of books.
Surely they are goodness within.
Thumb through the pages.
You'll feel the draft of wings.

Look at books as the giver of allowances
and you are holding out your hand.

Act like you know them all.
Gather their prairie grass in your arms.

Stomp dance in the library. Pow wow.

Tell the books they are brothers.
Say to them *You are relatives.*
Honor them with corn pollen on their noses.
Honor them with a star-quilt giveaway.

Tell them they are good medicine.
A buffalo herd snorting softly.

Say to the books *The war-ax of your pages cut.*

*You are rows of women making a tremolo for the warriors.*
I see the books as rows of horses carrying the warriors
into battle.
I hear the war cries of books.

Shout to the books like ships up and down
on the Great Atlantic.
The wide masts of their pages flapping.
Look at them like Columbus on the shore of America.
Look at the books as Natives meeting the ships saying
*They must be gods from heaven.*

Tell the books they are spirit-dancers.
Their pages are white flocks of birds.

Say *You heap big books.*
You boogie when there is no band.

Yes, shout to the books as if ships at sea.
Tell them they are coming to the new world.
Say they are Isabel sending us on a journey.

They are a table set for company full of white plates.
An after-dinner cigar.
Or the smoke of the peace pipe.

A spider carrying pieces of the sun in her web
to bring us light.

Say to the books *Your pages are snow-angels in winter.*
*A bushful of white blossoms in summer.*

Look at the library like a forest.
Or an elk herd grazing.

Think of it as a ship's log.
Or an intercessor saying *Have mercy. Look at the work*
*the people have done.*

Tell the library it is a *Grandmother* telling stories.
Without her words we do not live.

# Reconstructuring

I think sometimes this is what love is. The way I feel. Having language. Which is a view from space. It shows us *the other*. A vehicle to.

In the end it is the transference of tools that permit survival. Light the darkness. Clarify the essence of matter. It's another form of mythmaking. The myth telling that was. Is. And adding to it what you already are. The act of becoming. Colonizing with your voice. Wiping out confusion and uncertainty.

But I think sometimes I have to take the part of myself back. The times I tell him I'd rather work.

I remember standing at the window in the winter. Sometimes watching the heavy snows. Wanting to enter that white world. Thinking I could grow small and brittle but for the moving whiteness around me. The energy force I always felt from somewhere. But my life was still divided like the University of Minnesota I live a few miles from. The Mississippi River runs right through it. Separates the East Bank from the West. But the Mississippi is small up here. Not like say in St. Louis. Whatever that has to do with it. But I wanted to enter a world that was not divided into an outward and an inner life. I wanted the whiteness and energy of the world outside my window. And I wanted it inside myself.

I had to listen to myself who went unheard for years. Until it shouted. And I listened. It was full of loneliness. Ignorance. Unbearable sameness. Neglect. I had to leave the self-destructive behavior. What had I been doing? Killing a part of myself?

Becoming a traitor. The throwaway. That's what it was. The giveaway.

I wanted repatriation.

I think now love is what the energy force is.

The mornings I go on from the West Pole.

NOW

# Snow

It snowed one year in Minnesota on Halloween. By the next morning there were thirteen inches on the ground. By that afternoon twenty-eight had fallen.

When I pushed open the front door. Banging it several times with my weight before it would open. I knew the sweet smell of broken fir limbs. There was silence except for a high whine in the trees. The birds sat on the fence to be fed. They remembered last winter. But I didn't have birdseed.

Snowdrifts in the yard were higher than the twenty-eight inches that fell. I couldn't even wade through them. The snow was packed to the windows along the front of my house. The bushes opened to the sky. I shoveled one layer from the walk at a time.

There was news of cars and buses and snowplows stuck. It was Armistice Day, 1940. The last snow anyone could remember like it.

My yard had been full of leaves before the snow. I had raked some of them and put the sacks in the back of my new station wagon. I raked the others in a makeshift pile and drove to the Compost on Pierce Butler Route the afternoon it started to snow. But the Compost was closed on Thursdays so the leaves stayed in the back of my car in the garage.

You know sometimes you're caught off guard. Especially if you're from somewhere where there isn't much snow and they call you from Oklahoma laughing. Though some are worried. Your aunt who doesn't think you should have gone to Minnesota anyway. Though it's the best job you ever had. And you say you're all right. Though a depression comes with it. You remember the time in Iowa when you were there for a year and snow fell and the cold held on and you watched the birds shivering in the bush outside your window and you suddenly found yourself crying because of the harshness of the world. And how does anyone ever survive anyway except by an almighty hand?

When you're out shoveling you see the rabbit tracks and know the animals are hungry and as dismayed as you. You don't keep food for yourself in the fridge. Living in restaurants along college avenues because you cooked for years and now your family's grown and you don't want to do it anymore. And you can't get your car out of the garage. A snowplow came through the alley and packed it against the door and your car with leaves in it can't get out. You can't walk to the store a mile away because the street and sidewalks are full of snow. And it's like wading at the shore of a large ocean. You think of the old people and a friend calls. A man you dated and would still like to get back to you and he says he'll shovel your walk and take you to the store and out to eat. And you say okay. And you think of the people who have no one and you sink lower. Your head aches and you feel insignificant in the universe and what's wrong with that? You get a perspective in the snow. You think of dying and someone finding you days later. It never hurts to think of death. Snow reminds you of it. It keeps you from getting comfortable. You know how large the odds you're up against and you feel the veneer of civilization. But that's the way it is and your ancestors survived at least until they procreated and then the next generation and the next and here you are your children already out in the world and you can leave.

And the next day when the friend arrives you think *bless him* and you buy birdseed and some staples at the grocery and you think even in twenty-eight inches of snow that's nearly up to your parka in places where it's drifted and pulled all your bushes down. You'll be all right. All the way through winter into spring.

# Short Flight from Minneapolis to Chicago

You would think sometimes this wasn't meant to be. You wonder how we got here. And how things happen as they do. You think of the *infinite hand* that doesn't seem to care who it blesses but moves erratically and eventually at one time or another makes sense. You see the ice patterns frozen on a lake just after takeoff. Something random yet direct in following street patterns and plowing whirls like roads climbing hills. The cul-de-sacs underlying the ice. Lines quick and comb-toothed. Then higher in the air you see the sun's reflection on the ice field over a pond. You remember when all the earth was mud and the elk rolled over and left his hairs that became the prairie grasses. Only in snow you think it was the white bear and the shiny places of ponds are his fur worn to the hide. You think of the dynamic world and its chaotic behavior as you travel over clouds high above the same pattern almost as snow. You reconstruct your story of how it was the clouds that rolled in the mud and left part of themselves for the winter. And you like that version. Yes because we came from somewhere else. Somewhere above the earth. You feel it as you close your eyes and after a while the plane begins its descent. As you began long ago. You're glad the clouds are walls you can pass through. And you feel the plane drop blindly to earth. Yes of course on course through the clouds at least ten minutes and you still can't see the ground. You feel the plane's shaky equilibrium. You watch the rain streaks on the window as you lose altitude. You feel yourself drop through what feels like chaos. You are so close to the earth you finally break through the low gray ceiling of the sky. You look from the window and see the fingers of the runway reaching for you. And you see the earth shiny and wet as something brand new.

## *Louveciennes*, Camille Pissarro, Art Institute of Chicago

A man walks toward a bridge from a house much like you had with a yard through the trees.

Your head goes back to everyplace you've been. You think so anyway. The former husband. The snowy yard in *Louveciennes* like the white sheet of the bed you beat with your hands when he made you angry.

But it was you who left the house. Moved out. Though you barely made it. Maybe it was the Great Spirit's hand. Maybe a myth taking form. Like the cloth that flew and sank into the ocean and made the whales. You know how it is. You survive. When you look back. You don't know how.

Your companion walks through the gallery with you on a Sunday afternoon before your plane leaves from Chicago to Minnesota. You feel him though he's several paintings away and there are people between you.

And you see the weather you left in Minnesota is there in the painting. The kind of cold you feel up your nose. At eight below the windows crust. They are slices of bread you take from the freezer. You see the house in *Louveciennes* the man leaves. But it was you who carried the roof full of snow. The burdens that come with marriage. Then the divorce. You think of the thin streams of heat rising from houses. You see them up the street underneath the hard sun delivering its paper of cold light. The exhaust from cars.

You remember again it snowed the last night of October and kept on. Spreading over the yards like the salt plains you remember in Oklahoma. You see it there again at *Louveciennes*. The time you and the children needed help after you left him and he wouldn't give it. And you hit the white sheet hitting it and hitting it with your hands. Like a child. Or a man. Or like part of the human race.

## *Comanche*, Museum of Natural History, University of Kansas, Lawrence

*for Robert Gard*

It was after a hard day we followed rain on the Kansas Turnpike. We have it often out here. Pecking the windshield. Louder. Then softer. With a brief respite under the underpass. As if the wind suddenly stopped to take a breath.

And the clouds raised their white flags in the sky. And I thought of the horse I saw in the museum in Lawrence. After visiting my daughter. In her last year of law school at the university. And now my friend and I were returning to Minnesota.

The horse. Comanche. The only survivor of the Little Big Horn. June 25, 1876.

He stood in his glass case in Dyche Hall. With some drums and war clubs. Some sage grass and a few bleached bones. To give him the still-on-the-prairie look. His dark eye like a buckeye. His bridle marked *Seventh Cavalry*. His body restored with excelsior and wood and a few bones. His hide preserved in salt brine. The mount of Captain Myles Keough. A plaque explains.

The only living thing found on the battlefield by relief troops arriving two days later. The horses that could walk were led off by the Indians. Cheyenne probably though other bands gathered against Custer.

Now we pay toll at the end of the Kansas Turnpike, and I look for Highway 35 to take north to Minnesota nearly eight hours away and already it's five o'clock. And there off in the distance is Kansas City and the rain isn't falling except in big drops off the viaducts and under overpasses and what washes up from cars ahead of us.

We pass the refineries and storage silos like a tribe of ancestors. Then the old stockyards where my father came as a young man seventy years ago and lived his life and now it's over.

I wonder what it was like for Comanche that first and second night he lay on the prairie by himself. Maybe he heard the moans of the dying soldiers. He must have heard the Indians at their work of scalping and dismembering and gathering up what could be carried off as though the battle were over and the booty of boots and brass buttons and epaulets and war weapons and rifles were really theirs.

At first the sleet is delicate as a gourd rattle. As delicate as the rattle in a burnt-out lightbulb. A few miles later the sleet pecks harder.

The highway is fragile as the glass in a lightbulb. We expected fog in Iowa. Some icy roads. But we hear on the radio of the snow in St. Paul. Temperatures down to below zero. I watch the white line to stay on the road. My friend watches ahead for the red taillights of other cars.

Several hours later in Minnesota the highway is nothing more than a few ruts through the snow. I keep driving, thinking of the power of the ancestors.

When we get to St. Paul, I even make it up the hill on Randolph Boulevard. Make it within a block of my house. But my street has not been plowed and I have to leave my car in a snowbank at the end of the street. There's snow over the wheel wells and the car won't move. We walk through snow up to our knees. I feel it inside my boots and the legs of my trousers. I even struggle to get into the house through the snow packed against the front door.

We make several trips back to unload the car. Lifting our four feet through the snow. The dark sky over us. The moans of the dying storm around us. The white air of our breath among the war shields and war clubs and ghost drums.

# Minnesota Public Radio

I think there are many reactions to Thanksgiving among the Native Americans. And I think those reactions differ widely according to lifestyle. If the family is acculturated, if it works and lives in this world-that-is, a Thanksgiving dinner of turkey and stuffing is not out of the ordinary. I'm from a family, for instance, that had mixed heritage. My father was Cherokee. My mother English and German. We always had a turkey dinner with my mother's family. My father carved the turkey. I like Thanksgiving. It's a time for families. It's a time for thankfulness. It's a time to think about America, which is a formidable country because of its generosity to the world. Its commitment to peace despite its faults, especially injustice to the Native American. But I know many Native Americans don't share my feelings. There's bitterness over Thanksgiving. And rightly so, I think. There's opposition to any celebration of the white culture coming to the land. It marked the end of a way of life. How can the Native American celebrate defeat? How can anyone celebrate the robbery not only of land but of culture? How can anyone celebrate broken treaties and reservations? The extermination of millions of buffalo in a ten-year period? So there are many Native Americans, mainly the traditional ones, who do not celebrate Thanksgiving. My memories of this holiday were shared by the white members of my family. The Indian part was silent through all those years.

...

But if my Native American side did speak of celebrating Thanksgiving, if it were integrated enough into the white world, that is, to celebrate Thanksgiving, well, this is what the Indian part would say (possibly, anyway): Go into the woods and take your rifle. Find a plump turkey. Ask permission for his life. Shoot him quickly so he doesn't suffer. Honor him for the gift of his life. Give thanks also to the land. And to the Great Spirit, for game, and for making you a hunter. Pull out the feathers with the edge of your pocketknife. Slit the turkey to the breastbone. Stick your hand in to loosen the entrails. Cut off the neck. Remove the gizzard, heart, liver, and gallbladder, be careful not to break. Remove the oil gland from tail. Wash, stuff, and cook. But, well, that might not work if you don't live near the woods and you don't have a rifle. The next choice you have, therefore, is go to the Warehouse Market.

· · ·

Give honor to the building as you enter the door, though
you may not feel like it. Walk to the turkey aisle and look
through the bin.
Ask the spirits to guide you.
Praise the Great Spirit.
Honor the turkey with a song as you carry him to the
checkout line.
Take him home in a sack by himself.
He should not share his domain.
Remove the heart, liver, gizzard, neck.
On this kind of turkey they grow in a
plastic wrapper inside the cavity of his chest.
Think of your family as the turkey cooks,
and the blessing of the land.

· · ·

My son was in the Persian Gulf during the war, then stayed behind to pack equipment for shipment back to America. I think we had half the country over there. I remember the Thanksgiving I saw him after two years. After six months on the USS *Okinawa*, he told me how hard it was to stand when he first got off the ship. *You expect the land to move*, he said, *but it doesn't.*

. . .

I like to give voice to historical figures. The 102 passengers on the *Mayflower*, for instance. The hardship of their voyage.

I often travel across the land and pick up voices of my Indian ancestors. It takes more imagination to portray the white culture. But that's where our heritage is. In the head. Imagination. Vision. Memory.

*Nine weeks on the ship. The ocean tossed us like a child's shoe on the floor. It was always cold. Always shifting. I could feel the dampness on my hair. We had no way to wash. No place away from the others. We used a bucket—well, you can imagine. For every meal we ate pickled beef and cheese and hard dry bread. Sometimes we found worms. We had to stay in the cramped ship. The sea was too rough. The air. Even the drinking water was sour. I'm so tired of ocean. Of wind beating the masts all day. Give me the house I left with yellow light on the walls. The small blue table. A pear or apple in my bowl. I would have turned back if I could. Do you know how good it is to see land? If only you knew when you first step off a ship how hard it is to stand.*

And of course that first winter, half of them died. They buried their dead at night in hopes the Indians wouldn't know how weak and few they were. There was already mistrust.

And there was already pleading.

Just give us a little game and corn.

Just give us a little land.

# The West Pole

I think now the West Pole is Christmas. The end of the year. I always used to spend it with family. For fifty years, I went to Kansas City, Missouri, for Christmas. No matter where I lived. I was always there. But this year I stay in Minnesota. I was just back for Thanksgiving. Neither one of my children will be there. I decide to stay in my house. Alone on Christmas morning. No children rustling through packages. No relatives talking in the other room.

There are a lot of West Poles. The country growing older. The century. Myself. The browning of America or multiculturalism. Faith is a West Pole. Something not there unless you believe it is. America is the West Pole. We're at the end of the time zone, the latest continent toward which civilization moved. The West Pole is also the instability of the economy. The End of the Trail. All of it.

But this morning, the West Pole is Christmas. It is what you are inside yourself without anyone else around. I was with my parents when they died. It wasn't that they were alone. No more than I am alone this morning. They are all around me. The ancestors especially. I always feel them. My practical German mother would hit me in the head for that thought. But she isn't saying what I do anymore.

But I couldn't really be with my parents in their death, I guess. In the journey they were about to set out on. In that they were alone.

The feeling of loss. That's the West Pole. Certainly. There are times the loss sits on my chest like my cat. But that's why Christ was born. To give me strength when I have none. To take my burdens upon himself. Which I guess he did. I can go on. I can look at Christmas morning with no one but myself.

Maybe Christmas is a full circle. Birth and death joined.

I remember those early years of my divorce. I was already in my forties. Without practical skills. But I wanted out. These things are better left unsaid. Except to build a foundation for what I did.

I remember once when I was eating in Edmond, Oklahoma. I was working for the Arts Council then. Traveling to schools every week. There were some businessmen at the next table. I knew they had company cars and their rooms and meals were paid for by their companies and I was making much less and had all of that on my own. There is an anger here. It is a man's world. They hold the power. But I will not get bitter. I will thank the living God who has provided me with a living when all I could do was write and teach some. And who got me to Iowa where I received an M.F.A., on an Equal Opportunity Fellowship. And who got me to Macalester College where I have better work than with the Arts Council of Oklahoma. You can imagine.

When I face depression like I did Christmas Eve day. When I feel like sometimes I can't go on. I would say yes, it makes sense. Go fix some tea. Tomorrow it will be time to get up and go to work. In the meantime tell a story. Think how everything is connected. Remember how you felt close to your son when he was in the Persian Gulf. Remember the morning you woke dreaming of him. Only he was a boy with his hand in a fishbowl. You saw his hand stir the water. You looked at the fish. You saw how they had teeth. How they were swimming toward his hand. *Get your hand out of the water.* You woke as you were saying. And later, when you saw him again for the first time in nearly two years, he told you how on the ship they watched the screen for mines and missiles. You were with him even on the other side of the world.

That's where Christmas takes me at the end of the year.

# The Horse

There were probably animals in the manger that night. Camels and sheep, I guess. And donkeys. But nowhere is the horse mentioned in Bethlehem. But it's what I want to talk about a moment. Because to me that's the Christian faith. To have a horse. For years, centuries, I suppose, the Native American roamed this continent on foot. But then there was the horse. It came with the Spaniards from South America and Mexico. I suppose Christopher Columbus brought it on his ship. The horse had been extinct on this continent since the ice age. When the Native American saw the horse he called it the *Sacred Dog*. Or the *Medicine Dog*. It stood high as an elk but had no antlers. It changed the way of life. It came to define wholeness for the Native American. When two-rode-as-one. Or when the horse's shadow and your shadow were one. That's what it feels like to receive the light of Christ and ride on faith. You know the freedom from doing everything the hard way. On one's own strength. On foot, in other words. But with faith you have something to carry your burdens. You have something that goes on and on.

# A Christmas Memory

A man plays loud music in the next room. Last night I knocked on his door at twelve-thirty and told him to turn it down. I could hear him snore through the wall. In this place I can hear anything. Cars running. The birds. The crunch of boots. Someone stomping his feet against the curb. Someone coughing in his room. The building cracks with cold. Two days ago a winter storm covered the Great Plains. Moved east. Another one is coming. Now it's the end of the month just before Christmas. I wait for the roads to clear. I wait to get paid for my artist-in-residence job. At the Lone Ranger Motel in Edmond, Oklahoma, the world is not far away. The poor come in off the road. The men shift with construction jobs when they can find work. They talk by the thin Christmas tree and the gaudy-wrapped boxes in the motel office. Outside the gauntness of the hard sun on snow. Yesterday my Buick wouldn't start. I scraped snow and ice from the windshield. Then the hood until I saw scrape-marks on the paint. I should have left it alone. I should not speak of this room. The ugly television and wallpaper. The cheap French Provincial furniture that has nothing to do with anything. My cramps. The images I do not like are all here. The stupid chest of drawers. The shiftless people. The cars trying to start. The rapid music. The beat of it through the wall. Then the man gone. And the cradle of silence.

# The Drinking Vessel/A Christmas Gift

*for Kristi Wheeler*

What do you call this petrified canteen I unwrap in front of the fire? This bowl with its opening puckered to a spout? There's a feel of old in my hands. A shrunken bear head, two handles for ears, a high mouth for kissing the berries on a bush. Look at the markings like small bird feet. The old clay water jug is flattened on one side to ride against a horse or a hip. I think it was a woman's, not a hunter's or warrior's. Maybe she hung it on her shoulder as she climbed down from the cliff dwelling to hoe her row of corn. Maybe a hundred years passed while the vessel lay buried in sand or some caved-in kiva. How else could it survive to be sold in the flea market and unwrapped in my house? The log in the fireplace crackles. Tinsels of smoke rise from the black bark. The fire sounds like water crinkling inside the vessel as the woman fled the raiders, a whole civilization ghosting a clay vessel, this bowl with a mouth almost closed.

# You're Responsible for Your Own Leaves

There's snow on the ground. All winter. In Minnesota where I moved several years ago with my tumbleweed and lasso. The snow's piled up in the yards. Along the sidewalks and streets from November through April. Sometimes the heaviest snows come in April. You don't see the ground for five or six months. Sometimes you have to go back south just to see grass again. *But this is the ground in Minnesota*, a colleague said. You still have to forget the grass. It's gray sometimes for days. It gets meat-freezer cold. The sun barely comes through or the sky grows lighter but the heavy clouds return. They are always crossing. I don't know where they come from. Maybe the west and southwest just like in Oklahoma where I lived.

Leaving white veils of snow.

But you think ahead to some warm Sunday afternoon in May. The ground raw and damp. There's a chill in the air and you have to wear a sweater though after raking a while you have to take it off.

And someone will come to cut down the broken bushes. Open now to the sky. And these guests, these piles of snow, will go home. Back to the sky where they came from. And the trees will be trimmed and your tulips and jonquils will start to come up out of the ground. And the yard will be cleaned and vacant looking. Something new and raw as a bride.

# Television Is the West Pole

It's a story preserved with many voices telling it on their own channel, you see, sometimes associated with snow which some stories can only be told during.

Yo. TV's the new oral tradition. Continuing stories that alter our consciousness.

Have you had a house in which one room was empty? You didn't have furniture for it? That's what my heritage is like. An empty room. Maybe some curtains at the windows. Bookshelves empty. Whole histories unknown. Maybe the bed of a few stories you can rest in now and then. But the bed is narrow as the body that's on it. The spread a little rumpled. Wrinkles under you in the wrong place.

It's like having an invisible self to talk to. It's having an attic. And knowing you're part of the land. Like feeling full. Just after half a blackberry pie. The berries you picked yourself.

When I go to pow wows I get tears in my eyes watching those girls dance. I have to swallow and look somewhere else. I missed all that. I don't think they had pow wows in Arkansas anyway. My father was cut off from it. My white mother wouldn't allow it. All that noise and dancing. It would have taken away the isolation. That's what my childhood was. Living on the great ice cap. The frozen island of the ice blue light on the television in the dark. All the while moving. Migrating with the current. Kansas City to Indianapolis to St. Louis to Columbia to Tulsa to Kansas City to Tulsa to Iowa City to St. Paul. I spent most of my life packing and moving. Sometimes time goes by and I wake up and want to wad newspapers and wrap the dishes and box them up. Yes. I can hear the silverware like jingle dress. All fringed like well I don't know. Some things you got to leave unexplained. But the drumming and the stomping with the feet. It's tricky. You just don't get out there and do it. No. You have to feel it first. I don't dance. I just put my blanket on the hardwood floor in the empty room. I go to bed and can see the geometric patterns and the movement of something within me. Yes. That's where the Indian lives. In his (tele)vision. In the dance of unknown memory.

The West Pole is having the TV as a companion.

Then sometimes you hear the moon howl like a wolf over the next ridge. Aoooooooooo. Aoooooooooo. Like that. You know. Aooooo all night. And you know the moon's only a reflection of the sun. Yes. With those stars. I want to see that moon when it comes out. Yes I do. Opening with the picture show of the stars in town. Sometimes full face. Sometimes looking out behind the door of her room. There in the night sky. You know we don't know anything. Whole worlds are going on here and we don't always know it. Yes that's what we get from thinking we're so smart. Just chugging on our own little trail each day.

I tell you my life reads like a road map.

And what does the world look like through blue eyes?

Yes, sometimes I feel like packing up. Someday I'll move again. Right off this earth. Soon I'll be up there like one of those shiny marble stars. Just slick as breath.

# HISTORY

# Comment

History can now be seen as the writing of one's own story into the fabric of the written text. Maybe even the *rewriting* of one's own story into the *rewritten* text. In the context of feminist and minority writing, I'm thinking now of history in terms of *chewing the language*. I'm thinking in terms of *Macenattowawin* (birch bark biting). The women who put their teeth into their work. The white bark is peeled from the birch. The layers pulled apart. A piece folded in half and then half again. A woman named maybe *nvuelzjch* taking the point of it in her mouth. Biting along the fold. Eyeteeth against side teeth. She chews a geometric design in the papery bark. A braille of sorts. Something like a large snowflake when she unfolds it. Maybe the pattern of woodland blizzards still in her head. The old woman has chewed so long her teeth are gone. The spirits come to her in bifocals. Together they enter the chaos before creation. They feel their way back through the dark. The birch-bark biter hears the ancestors in their graves. Sometimes they grind their teeth in sleep. She holds to the spirit ahead of her. Her dentures chewing. Does it matter the earth has changed? *nvuelzjch* still has the journey. Bringing her bitings back from the dark.

# A Short Historical Perspective of the Native American in a Nonhistorical Book

There's a strange story long ago of an Indian woman mourning her son. I don't remember the tribe. She walked along the edge of the water. Suddenly she looked up. She saw two spruce trees in the water. She saw ropes tied to the trees. Then a bear stood up. It looked like a bear. But it had the face of a man. The woman returned to her village and said *My son is dead and the thing we have heard about is on the shore.* As if the two were connected. The bear-men put their hands to their mouths and asked for water. The Indians set fire to the two spruce trees. With boxes down in them. The floating land with spruce trees. It burned like fat. Tribes came to see the two men-faced bears. They kept them in separate villages. That is the end of the story.

Before Columbus there's an old history of visits to this continent from others. Trips to others from ours. But in the new history we come closer to understanding—

Years before the white man came to Turtle Island, there was a civilization that stretched across our continent. A largely unknown civilization the center of which was Cahokia, Illinois, just east of St. Louis. Possibly A.D. 700 to A.D. 1100. Its population was about thirty thousand Indians. A large earthen mound remains. Over 100 feet high. With other smaller mounds. And there's a museum now too.

The Cahokia civilization disappeared about five hundred years before the pilgrims came. Possibly from disease. There were trade patterns all over the hemisphere. Maybe they just migrated for a reason we don't know. The old civilization just packed up and went somewhere. As if the inhabitants of Cleveland, for example, would suddenly leave the city.

The white man came to the dark ages of Turtle Island and never knew it. That's when the brilliant light Christopher Columbus stubbed his toe somewhere to the southeast of us. There along the shelf of ocean. The space and resources. He didn't even know it yet. But who could not think what he saw was there for the taking?

It was a land the Peacemaker had blessed. Long ago. Dekanawida established a Five Nation Confederacy and the Iroquois constitution. Somewhere between A.D. 1000 and A.D. 1400. About the time the Cahokia Mound Builders were closing up in the center of Turtle Island, on the northeast coast, a leader the Indians called the *Peacemaker* established some laws so the different tribes could get along. The Indians nominated and voted on their leaders. The women had a voice in government. Wrong leaders could be removed. The whole thing sounding familiar. But this guy Columbus. The ancestors must sit on their stars and ask *Who's that?*

Without doubt America thrived under the Peacemaker's blessing. America continued the Confederacy. They called it their own name. *Democracy.* They had their own style of it. But we knew the tune.

Now this is the creation myth of America—

At one time there was a sky rock and the animals who lived on it started falling off to the water below because it got crowded up there. The animals on the sky rock worried about falling. They knew they would drown in the water below. So they sent the water beetle down and he swam to the bottom of the water and brought up some mud to the surface and it grew and spread and became dry land. It was named *Turtle Island. The-dry-land-that-floated. The-hard-ground-for-those-drowning-in-water.* Though later it was called *America.* It still offered a solid place in the world.

What is there to say about Native American history? Assimilation or Annihilation. Those were the choices. A history of removal trails. A history of attacks on wagon trains with their flopping tops. In turn, a history of a slow and brutal conqueredness.

There were the 1778-1871 treaty years, which was mainly the 1832 Removal Act for the Southeastern Five Civilized Tribes, and the nineteenth-century *get-rid-of-them* years for the Northern Plains.

After the treaties, for the Plains Indian, there was the 1876 Little Big Horn. The 1885 Land Allotment Act to make farmers of migratory Plains Indians. The government handed out some land and said *Plow*. By 1890 the Plains Indian knew he wasn't a farmer. There were Ghost Dances at Wounded Knee. Someone named Wovoka said to dance and the buffalo and ancestors would return. And the Seventh Cavalry opened fire.

Then the twentieth-century attempts to revitalize the dark ages or silences of Native culture. The smudge of nonhistory or unrecognized history.

Just a few. 1924—Citizenship and the right to vote. 1932—The Relocation Act. Moving reservation Indians to urban areas. 1934—The Indian Reorganization Act. Instituting a tribal government of elected chair and council. 1953—The Termination Act in which reservations were terminated to bring the Indian into mainstream America. Which failed also. The 1978 Religious Freedom Act. The gradual awareness that help had to come from within. The cry for responsibility. Not dependency.

It's been the same cry for the Five Civilized Tribes, especially the Cherokee. Economic independence. Stability despite political turmoil. A sense of wholeness for a historically mixed-blood, hybrid people who were separated by clans. Sometimes Indian, sometimes white.

The Cherokee had been hunters and warriors, then farmers in Georgia and corners of other southeastern states, until their removal to Indian Territory in the 1830s. The Cherokee spoke a different language than the other four tribes, the Creek,

Choctaw, Chickasaw, and Seminole. The Cherokee language had its roots in the Iroquois.

They were a woodland tribe, wearing turbans and tunics and homespun pants. Some wore deer leggings and beaded belts. The women made calico dresses. They roasted corn and potatoes. The Cherokee adopted the white man's ways because they wanted the iron pots, the fish hooks and knitting needles. They were an educated and complicated people, a mix of superstition and Christianity, who spent as much time in Washington as professional lobbyists and delegates as they did on their own land.

But in the end, the same thing happened to them that happened to the Plains Indian who did not adopt the white ways. In fact, it happened to the woodland tribes first. No matter what anyone did. The *spruce trees* and the *bear men* with their hands to their mouths had arrived.

# Columbus Meets Thelma and Louise and the Ocean Is Still Bigger than Any of Us Thought

Jeez Louise.

There were countless Quincentennial articles on Christopher Columbus and his discovery of the New World. (1) He was a true zealot who dreamed of saving souls for heaven. A real evangelist who risked the trip of conversion. (2) He was a dud looking for Glory. Recognition. Gold. A fame-dancer. Exploiter. (3) Or he was a human being full of, well, Bravery, along with self-interest. A true Human Being. He faced a new frontier half-afraid he'd fall off the earth. But the Old World needed a lot of spices and slaves and stuff. And he was the one to do it. (4) Or he was a Jew fleeing Spain. Yes. There had been an Inquisition. Maybe C.C. was Jewish as some have proposed. (5) Maybe he just needed to get away for a while. (6) Or maybe he was sent by his wife who had connections with the court. Her father had maps or something. They already knew the earth was round anyway. So Columbus went as a common surveyor. Just to prove them right. (7) Or he was the great discoverer. The visionary who had a mission we have misinterpreted and was really (8) Christopher Columbus, the first feminist.

It was the 1991 movie *Thelma and Louise* that shed light on this proposal.

Yes, I posit that Columbus was the forerunner, the archetype, of the new woman who sheds her boundaries, enters the updated caravel of the green Thunderbird, and sails across the Southwest, a mere symbol of the ocean solidified, the new literary text.

Actually, the new woman didn't have much choice. Mainly undervalued. Enough of the Old World had been enough.

So Columbus sailed the liquidity. He was one of the first ones we know to be *out there*. Because of him Thelma and Louise have footsteps to follow.

Columbus offered a paradigm shift. And left a codified *diario* of how to do one's own naming. He took possession of the land. Misnamed the people there. He welcomed the Indians to the Indies. Called them what they weren't. In his diaries he seems almost the arriver and the one greeting the arrived.

Because of Columbus I have a name I am not.

He presented his own set of values. His own way of claiming. I can do that too in this world he left.

At least the New World was never the same after he came. Actually it was an Old World with a developed civilization that was wiped out by disease, dissolution, and, on the North American continent, the loss of the buffalo, which was the source of life: food, hides, medicine, bow strings, and so forth. That's really what Columbus marked. The discovery of the West Pole. The downshift of civilization on this continent, especially for the Native American.

And wasn't he a feminist, keeping his two diaries as he crossed the ocean? One for himself, the other for public view, telling his men that they hadn't made as many miles as they had, in case they were in for a long trip. *Mother Columbus* telling his men that everything was all right. They would be there soon.

His own diaries are retold by Fray Bartolome de Las Casas and translated by two men, Oliver Dunn and James E. Kelley Jr. In the copy I bought anyway. (*The* Diario *of Christopher Columbus's First Voyage to America 1492-93*, University of Oklahoma Press, 1989.)

In fact, the cover says de Las Casas "abstracted" the diaries.

Interpreted them in his own way. What woman can't relate to that?

martes .25. de setiebre
Avrian andado aq̃l dia al gueste 4 leguas y media y en la noche al su deste 17 leguas q̃ son .xxi. puesto q̃ de[z]ia a la gente 13 leguas /. porq̃ siemp finxia [?] a la gente q̃ hazia poco camino: porq̃ no les pare çiese largo /. por maȓa q̃ [?] escrivio por dos caminos aq̃l viaje : el menor fue el fingido : y el mayor el Vrdadero /. anduvo la mar mỹ llana por lo qual se echarõ a nadar mũchos marineros. (p. 42)

Tuesday 25 September (1492)
They had gone that day about four leagues and a half and during the night 17 leagues southeast, which makes 21, though he told the men 13 leagues, because he always pretended to the men that they were making little way so the voyage would not appear long to them. So he wrote that voyage in two ways: the shorter was the pretended; and the longer, the true. The sea became very calm, because of which many sailors went swimming.

Then comes the line:

The sea became very calm, because of which many sailors went swimming.

Yes, Columbus took power over his own body and his own sea, and others went swimming in it.

Namely Thelma and Louise.

I think their story is an example of the palimpsest. Writing over the invisible text of what really was.

Taking the journals and opening the erasures. Is following Columbus's wake. Is moving west.

Now *Mother Columbus* is taking care of his new stepchildren, the Indians. In some places ordering the Indians to come aboard. In others disembarking. Offering them glass beads and mirrors. The gift-bearing mother. Pretending to be interested in them on their level.

*Stepmother* Columbus turning cruel when they didn't bring him enough gold.

Yet they called him God. *God-mother* Columbus. Though strangling their life. Taking more than he gave. Maiming and killing them while saving them.

Crone Columbus.

The forerunner of Thelma and Louise. Shooting up trucks. Leaving men dazed in their tracks.

How can it be bypassed? The male-dominated world is the Texas we're not going through. Nevertheless, they find themselves in the pinnacled landscape. The natural spires of the Southwest. The power of the tower.

*It's a good thing you're not regional manager, Thelma,* you never would have made it to the road.

But here you are Columbus getting ready for his voyage, taking *the lantern, Louise, because we're going to have some light here.*

*So, Louise, will you take care of this gun?*

*Well put it in my purse, Thelma, good Lord.*

*I've never been out of town without Daryl.*

But now Thelma is in the truck-stop cowboy two-step bar and ballroom. We see seasick Thelma vomit at the *Silver Bullet,* or *Silver Pellet* or *Pullet,* or whatever the name of the cow palace where they stop to kill the oppressor.

*We need to get you some fresh air, Little Lady.*

Yes, murder is the first step. The dissolution of the Old World as it disappears on the horizon.

And now you're onto the glories of the open sea.

And Louise, too, is seasick alongside the road as she steps outside the caravel a moment. Realizing the full-sail of implications.

Then it's true flight on four wheels. The whole sea of the Southwest for the journey. Actually it's a study in the literary text.

Setting out for new ground.

Not interpreting the same old way, i.e., the text as its single authority.

It's women who live in two worlds, the public and private, working with the chromatic, the alternative tuning of instruments.

The inward personal layered saying-of-one-thing-and-meaning-another. Apparent form, hidden meaning. Emerging and bleeding genres. Studies of silences. How to lie and keep secrets. Present the unsure as what is sure.

Thelma and Louise couldn't tell their itinerary, you know, or they'd be tracked down. And they were escaping closure in the new process of discovery.

C.C. just began the journey. He was not actually able to discover that the earth is indeed flat and you can fall off. No, leave it to the women to make that discovery.

But he tried. It's just that land kept getting in the way. In his frustration alone he was a feminist.

Yes, Thelma and Louise carry on where men have failed and actually discover the end of the earth. Landlessness. And sail off.

No, the first feminist, Christopher Columbus, alone couldn't do it. He was too bogged with land. Unfortunately he kept running into. But he paved the way.

There are passages of domestic sensitivity in his diary:

Wednesday 17 October (1492)
And I saw that some ships' boys traded a few small pieces of broken pottery and glass for javelins. And the others who went for the water told me how they had been in their houses and that inside they were well swept and clean and that their beds and furnishings were made of things like cotton nets. The houses are all made like Moorish campaign tents, very high and with good smoke holes, but I did not see among the many villages that I saw any that surpassed 12 to 15 houses. Here they found that the married women wore cotton shorts; the young girls did not, except some who were already 18 years of age. And there were dogs,

mastiffs and terriers. And there they found a man who had in his nose a piece of gold which was something like half of a *castellano*. I rebuked them because they did not trade for it.

There are personal and passionate passages:

Friday, March 15 (1493)
Much of the time that I was in Your Highnesses' court, I met with the opposition and contrary opinion of many important persons of your household, who were all against me, alleging my enterprise to be ridiculous. I hope in Our Lord that it will be the greatest honor to Christianity that, unexpectedly, has ever come about.

His palinode still sings today.
Every woman knows it in the recognition of herself.
*It's all right, Louise, let them take your life savings.*
*But it's not all right, Thelma.*
But Louise, remember how tough our matriarch, Columbus, had it. We'll just ask for the assets of the court at the next Quick-Trip stop and make for the open sea.

It's just a matter of deciding *fuck yourself, Daryl*. Get in your ship and go. You have authority to make your own way.

Take the captainship in your own hands. Hear the text. Take it into consideration. Deconstruct. Perceive in your own way. Rebuild with your own *facing of the edge*. Then accelerate.

Yes, right there in the motel room, I swear, when Louise is on the phone to Jimmie, there's an Old World map on the wall.

The Atlantic full of water. A new coast somewhere.

Then later, when Thelma says *I can't go back. Something in me has crossed over.* Well, you see the little brown ships of her eyes.

Maybe it took centuries, but it's women coming into their own journey after Columbus. No. Making their own world to journey in.

*Can I go with you?* Jimmie asks.
*It's not a good idea right now* Louise says.

125

*But I'll catch up with you later. After I find the edge of the earth and how to fall over it, escaping from roles too small into the self-determined text.*

And once I envision the voyage nothing is ever the same.
Driving day after day
even to the roadbed of an empty sea.

# Hollyhock (A *personal* of my own life history)

On a walk I pass hollyhocks in a yard. I remember them on my grandfather's farm in Kansas. Several acres of his fields spread out. The barn, sheds, like pebbles of memory. My grandmother's farmhouse, staunch, white, her hollyhocks in the front yard. An outpost on the prairie where a man and wife raised four children, survived making bread, tending animals, weeding, sewing quilts for winter. Stocking the smokehouse, cellar. Snow and sun year after year. The giant hollyhocks on their stalks. Rough-stemmed with a stub of messy pollen. The red petals crinkled as old campfires. I always picked them at the farm. They were from another world, flaming and serene. A reminder there was something more than chores and farmwork. There was something more than this.

# An Infrequent Journey

There were many trips to my mother's parents' farm when I was growing up. There were few trips to my father's mother's place in Arkansas.

My father's people are buried in Hand Cove Cemetery above Norfolk Lake in northern Arkansas. When Orvezene, or Jene, my grandmother, was young, and the river was dammed, and the lake covered their farm, my grandmother and her eight brothers and sisters signed the sale of their land with X's.

My grandmother married William Jasper Hall, a country doctor in Viola, Arkansas. He was thrown from a horse and died. Afterwards she raised two children until my father was old enough to go north to Kansas City for work and send money back to her and his sister, Effie. It was in the last ten years of my grandmother's life that I knew her.

I still have the image of the backseat of my father's car. A narrow, winding road through the hills. A lake crossing on a ferry. An Indian woman. Not a birch bark biter. Not a history of ancient travel back and forth across the Bering Strait. But a fog, something like the fog that could fill the valleys between the Arkansas hills. A fog that came from the loss of the past, as well as from vapor and the smoke of woodstoves.

I still have the image of a flat plank floor somewhere. A rustle of little people under the house. A history of *coveringup* what I wasn't there to remember, but carried with me as though I was.

My grandmother's silence stirred in the leaves on the large trees that surrounded her place. In that silence, the whole unspeakable world turned. Much of it I have added from life that came after those visits, as if they were an insect strip—

My father's mother's place was somehow far away and deep and unknown. Evils lurked in the world. Little people could magically move things around. What you were sure of, you couldn't be sure of at my grandmother's place. There were small elements in a larger box where there had been ovens that baked people, where there were horrors on a scale that horrified the mind. Made it a hotbox of pressure that *spilledout* in dreams of red lava and men, though later, they would look sad and small back there in history, buy they could still bite off my nose.

My grandmother had come from a removed race. Soldiers had even tried to exterminate the buffalo. The spirit animal of our country that was supposed to be from my Indian past but wasn't. Making the uncertainties more uncertain.

My grandmother's place in Arkansas was a big, unknown country my mother didn't like. Farther away across the ocean in other countries things had happened. They also had happened in our own country though we tried not to look. And they still would happen despite courtrooms and God in heaven saying *It shouldn't happen.* But as long as there were roads into Kansas and Arkansas, which returned to Missouri where we lived, as long as my father's hands were on the wheel, as long as I felt the hard edge of their love, I was somehow safe.

# Photo Album

Our house on Woodland in Kansas City faced the west. Each day the sun pushed its way onto our front porch and into the house.

I had a tricycle.

When I was three my brother was born.

We went to church.

We went to the farm.

I was given piano lessons.

I was a campfire girl.

When I was eight I got a Schwinn.

I had the idea from my parents that things should be done right.

We lived in America. My father voted Republican. My mother was a Democrat.

She made pot roast, mashed potatoes, and apple pie.

My father went to work each day.

They married in the Depression, but waited until it was over to have two children.

There was something in their lives that was not fun.

My father was dark and my mother light.

She was angry when I played in the sun.

Something was not explained. Something not told. What we wouldn't talk about was the way to make it go away.

I had a hunger for story. A hunger for words.

I did nothing to know I would someday teach, lecture, travel, write, or read my words to anyone.

It looked like there was nothing down the road.

But inside something said I lived on the Great Plains of America. From the West Pole each day a light pushed itself into the house. I would look back someday. I would get through.

Using Photos to *Story* as if They Were Teepee Drawings of
Personal/Tribal History (As if Having a Teepee)

*Anna Myrtle Adams Wood,
my maternal grandmother,
circa 1904*

*Orvezene Lewis Hall, my paternal grand-
mother, circa 1907*

*Lewis Hall, my father, 1911*

*Edith Wood, my mother, 1913*

*My father with his mother, Orvezene, and his sister, Effie,
1936*

*My grandmother Orvezene and her pigs, 1940s*

The hollyhocks on my grandfather's farm, circa 1935,
Forest and Myrtle Wood,
my maternal grandparents,
Lewis and Edith Hall, my
parents, Aunt Martha Wood,
Uncle Carl and Aunt Mil Wood

My parents, 1934

*My father and me ready for my first trip, May 1941*

*The tricycle, my mother, and me, June 1941*

*My father and me on my first war horse, August 1942*

*"Farther away across the ocean in other countries things had happened." Aunt Mil and Uncle Carl Wood*

*Me, age 5*

*Me and my brother, David, 1947*

*Each day the sun from the
west, 1948*

*"Something was there
in knifing buckshot from
the bird or animal."
On the farm, 1949*

*On the farm, 1949*

*The back of our house in
Kansas City, 1949*

*The Sunday school class, 1949*

*The Schwinn, 3/18/1949*

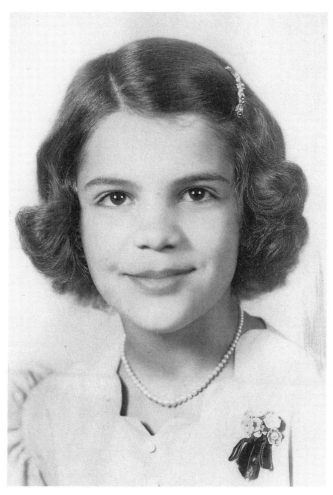

*Me, probably about 10*

*"We went to church." My
brother and me, 1952*

*"My father carved the turkey." Thanksgiving 1958*

*My senior picture, Normandy High School, St. Louis,*
*1959*

*Writers' conference in Freiburg, 1992*

*The Companion at the Danube in Regensburg*

*Beckers Butte above the Salt River Canyon, Arizona, 1993*

*Marine First Lieutenant David Glancy, my son, on board the USS* Okinawa
*during the Persian Gulf War, 1992*

*My daughter, Jennifer Glancy, graduation, University of Kansas, 1990. (Photograph by Jan Hall)*

*War Horse II*

# Sugar Woman

*for P. T. Vance*

> My heart is red and sweet.
> Sitting Bull

1.

Columbus came for gold. He wanted to find India and trade spices. He had almost nothing to do with the principles on which America was founded. That was mainly England. And the pilgrims nearly two hundred years later.

But Columbus thought the world was round, and if he sailed west, he'd come to India. He just didn't realize there was another continent and ocean in the way. But he called us Indian anyway. He didn't listen, but went ahead. That strong-headed, red-blood movement toward a goal despite obstacles is part of America. Putting a big foot onto the world. Forging ahead. Even before Copernicus and Galileo somewhere on rooftops above the night-blue streets of Poland and Italy looked up into the skies and thought there was a good chance we were the ones who moved. Didn't those kind of people burn at the stake? Yet they insisted the world was not flat. Columbus sailed because of it.

So in thinking of Christopher Columbus as the discoverer of America, we recognize someone who stumbled onto our land, or a little south of it, to be exact. Nonetheless, after Columbus, the steady flow of traffic from the east did not let up. There had been the Vikings. Maybe the Phoenicians. Who knows who else. But they left and not much changed. It was different with Columbus. His arrival marked the end of one time and the opening of another. It was the start of the West Pole for the Indian. After Columbus, the white man would keep coming and forever change the life of the Native American.

2.

So what of the arrival of Columbus?
Well, like the Chippewa story of maple sugar
things would get harder.

At one time, according to a Chippewa tradition
it used to rain syrup under the maple trees.
All you had to do was stick out your tongue.
And you know how the Indian loves sugar.
But the Trickster decided that was too easy.
He said the Chippewa would get lazy.
The Trickster said the Indian should work for his sugar.
An offering of tobacco had to be made.
Fires built.
It should take a little patience and worry.
A little sweat.

So the Trickster taught the Chippewa
how to stick a hollow twig into a maple tree
so the sap would run out.
He taught them to collect the sap into birch bark buckets.
He showed the Indian how to cut and gather wood.
He taught them to make a rack
and light a fire underneath.
He taught them how to keep the fire burning
and to boil the sap for a long time.
This kept them from being idle.

1.

For 156 years, from 1620 to 1776, the United States gradually developed a sense of law and self-government. The Magna

Carta. England's Parliament. A lot of things. Certainly some ideas of government also came from the Iroquois. Wasn't it Ben Franklin who said that if self-government could work for the savages, it could work for the American colonists?

There were some Visionaries. Real Human Beings, if you want. Some in Philosophy. The Enlightenment. The Individual going Somewhere. A contract with government for that going.

Most of our Visionaries were in Politics. George Washington. Thomas Jefferson. Madison. Hamilton. Whoever else wrote the Declaration. The Constitution. The Removal Act. The opposite joint of Democracy and Capitalism.

There should be said something about the English Language. Christianity. But that is enough for now.

2.

So the life of the Native American moved west.
No longer
would our ancestors be from the great salt-waters
toward the rising sun.
Now we faced the other direction.
The northern tribes as well as the southern.

To escape the new people that came.
To be removed to land west of the Mississippi
where my own tribe, the Cherokee,
along with the other four civilized tribes
could be safe and reestablish themselves
as corn farmers.

The northern migratory tribes moved also
to follow the ever diminishing herds
across the plains.

Hunger, disease, disheartedness, landlessness,
starvation, assimilation, annihilation.

1.

But the new America moving forward had Economists and Moral Philosophers. Adam Smith said we could be selfish because the invisible hand would produce good for the whole country.

That's the wealth of the nation.

The people in the industrial age could make all the hay forks they wanted. But the best hay fork at the least price would sell. With most of the buyers saying what's sold and who it is that sells.

That's why Capitalism. But it has to be law enforced.

And there have to be morals between people to do right. The invisible bonds that basically do to other people what you do yourself.

2.

But without discovery
would not have happened what happened.
The colluvium of two worlds.
The running amok.
Discovery had to be.
What would we have been without it?
Without the blood flushing the Native American.
Fucking us up and down.
TaKING the land.
Folding up our winter counts.
Givingus the dark ages.
It was going to be one of them.

Why not England with its brussel sprouts?

1.

Yes, it takes a Christian Conscience for Capitalism to work. And the Equality of Democracy.

A Citizen has to judge his own actions the same way he judges Others. He has to pursue his own economic self-interest for the good of the group.

But what when there is wrong? And the Bible says there is.

So Capitalism only works with people being civil. Having conscience. Respecting the law. The others. It doesn't work by itself alone.

So what do you do with the evil in human nature?

2.

There in vacation Bible school
where my mother sent me.
Did not Jesus love the Sheep?
The sugar maple Christ who called himself Word.
Who washed the evil hand.
Is worth a case of soda pop
and all the sugared Toast'ems you can eat.

1.

Eminent Domain. Manifest Destiny. It was going to happen. What other nation would you rather have? Russia with its colossal economic failure and disregard of human dignity? Japan with its lack of individuality?

Communism is economic failure because the law of supply and demand is put in reverse. Ideology and the state decide what is made where and for whom the broom.

The Japanese identify with their nation's central planners for the good of the country and for centuries doused the freedom. Brutal to the individual.

If America has to be, then let it have its big foot. Let it step unasked into the world. Democracy and Capitalism and Christianity. Let the American Work Ethic and Human Rightists speak.

2.

So I have a stick stuck in my bark.
My sap's gathered in the birch bark bucket.
Boiled until it turns syrup.
The syrup boiled until it's granulated.
Until it's maple sugar.
Until I'm sweet roses and solid as the icing's cake.
Am I not licked?
My elbows and ears.
Between my fingers.
Without discovery would I have had?
The telling of the stories which have disappeared?
It is enough.
How long have I spoken of what I live without?

Good-bye is what I had.

You know when Spring came
the Chippewa moved to the maple trees.
Built fire racks for the iron kettles
they traded for.
(Ten beaver skins for one kettle.)
You know the hot under the pot.
The gathered-up-sap from trees.
I'm now boiling sap.
All kettles on fire.
You see the heat runs up my legs
into my belly
up into the hollows of my lungs
out my mouth in hot words.
I sing to Jesus *Save me.*
Sometimes there're little holes in my flesh.
Pour some syrup in.
It hardens into candy and granulates into maple sugar.
Just boil it long enough.

1.

But the invisible hand doesn't mean you can do anything you want and everyone will profit. Human nature which is the central self sucks in with all its lungs and takes what is KING. Even the Indian would you know.

So now they are in trouble and we can watch their Wounded Knee. Our country has lost its conscience. Now America is the economic war. What you put on others is what you get you see.

2.

The anger rises.
That's what I wouldn't have without discovery.
Possibly wholeness.
Possibly land.
Come on. What am I griping about?
Just because I lost my hide-scraper?
But it was more than that.

In vacation Bible school
I saw the tabernacle fire boiling maple sugar.
Am I not sweet?
Does not everyone stick out their tongue when I pass?
Then clean a space for this New
coming horribly in ships and wagons
and Cherokee chiefs.

The English words are also Beings in themselves.
The bodies and spirit-transformations of them.
I speak the new language now.
My heart is Jeep-red and sweet.

They suck me don't they?
I feel a lot of tongues.

# NOW

# War Horse I

I have a new car now. But for thirteen years I drove a brown Buick station wagon. It had 184,555 miles when I gave it to a friend. You know I think I left my husband more easily than I left that car. Toward the end I cried when I had to look for another car. But it wouldn't pass the emissions test. I asked an Indian friend what he was going to do with his Indian car. He said there wasn't a test on the reservation and he could keep his car. He asked what I was going to do with the Buick. He could use it for hunting. As soon as I had a place for it, I could think of another car. The first key I had for it bent from turning the ignition all those years. They almost never got a new key made. I remember when I saw the car in Tulsa, Oklahoma, in 1978. I knew it was mine. I don't live in Oklahoma anymore but I remember it on the back roads there. Driving Highway 62 to Altus, Oklahoma, when it must have been 105. No air. Sitting on Mount Scott near Lawton. Driving to the Black Mesa that reaches New Mexico. My children grew up in that car. Everyone said it would never start in Minnesota when I moved. But it did. I got a small truck battery and we went through the snow. I cleaned out the glove compartment when the car went to the Fond du Lac Reservation without me. Insurance papers with eight addresses in three different states. A few invoices for new brakes, a transmission, tires. A whisk broom, an air gauge, a bulb for the rear light, a few maps. A Bible with curled pages under the front seat. Nothing in the trunk but two ice scrapers and some rope I used to tie things on top of the car once in a while. A 1978 Buick Estate Wagon. Serial number 4R35X8X153975. Brown as a war horse.

# War Horse II

The next time I see my old car is in the movies. Yes. You won't believe it. But there's this film. This documentary. *With Reservations*. And my old car is in it. Showing up like a big shot. Next to the moose hanging on the scaffolding after hunting season. The Indian friend, who has my car now, starting to dress the moose. And the car there as if it had a part in the hunt. As if maybe it held the bow and arrow. Just like when you go to the Hunting Grounds you are new again and the old way of life returns as if you'd never had to do without it. Yes. I know someday I'll see the car again on the highway. We'll pass as if old friends. Did not our heart burn within us? The disciples asked when Christ passed them on the road after the resurrection. They were going somewhere talking with their friends. And he just passed. Yes sometime I'll be going somewhere and my old car will come up from behind and pass me the way I know sometimes my father has been beside me. Only I didn't know it until the moment he left.

# War Horse III

Faith is a vehicle. I guess. I got through anyway by believing. When I was boxed in with circumstances stronger than me. Somewhere I knew there was a state of release. I believed fear and hopelessness weren't a permanent state even when they looked like they were.

In a way, the West Pole is Industrialization. Moving on now under someone else's power. Not the harvest of my own hands like Cain tried in the Bible. But acceptance for the Old Testament God, anyway, was through the blood of a lamb. It was Abel who somehow knew it was up to something else.

The other night before I went to sleep you know, I saw a test pattern in my head. I don't know how to explain it. A cross between microchips and the layout of maybe the Cahokia Mounds, with orbits—but not that either.

There were rings of circles, each one bigger than the other. Like so many bowls of Mammy Yokum's pipe. From many different perspectives. But the rings were not lines, but maybe small specks. Or something. A square mound in the middle. A line running from corner to corner to four other smaller mounds. As though an almost invisible X crossed the circles, but was at the same time one with them. Yes, there were little square mounds on each of the four corners of the test pattern. And maybe some between the larger one in the middle and the corner ones.

The West Pole is also something primitive.

Then there was another pattern after it. One moving. Something like the curl of smoke from Mammy Yokum's pipe when she takes a lot of puffs.

But ordered too.

You always want to diversify power. Guarding and checking and balancing the other. You always want to step beyond.

You want to have a test pattern after the program goes out.

# THREE REVIEWS

# Comment

I'm ready for a return to *horse sense*. Some sort of further *Coyosmic* theory called *Mammy Yokum's Relativity*. A *New Pragmatism*. Moving truths within Truth. A kinetic common-sensed *multiform-ality* giving all things voice. Yet valuing the technique of *other*.

The freedom to move between them at different times in differing modes.

A radiant multimigration. A changing pragmatism with room for ambiguity and ambivalence. A new negative capability filled with gasoline.

A more mobile *Mothernity* accepting differing offspring. Able to cook all sorts of things on backyard kettles. Able to maneuver in combat boots.

Able to stomp dance and bugaloo. Or "grass dance and bunny hop," as Louise Erdrich writes in *Love Medicine*. Able to operate as variables. As the *beads* in that same book. As a coyote, shape-changer series of images. The beads as a rosary around a young girl's neck. As a means of Indian art (beading). As a symbol that connects both white and Indian worlds. As pebbles rolled in a streambed until they're smooth. The beads as the people themselves whom life has rolled over and over in its streambed. The beads could even represent Indian gambling stones. They could be the string of stories, or chapters, strung in a line. A circle. Beginning and ending at the same crossroads. Or stops at a series of bus stations. They are a symbol that holds two worlds (the physical and spiritual). Because of human needs, don't the Indians make small tobacco ties on a string like a rosary for the sweat lodge ceremony? Don't the Catholics roll the beads with their fingers, entering communication with the spirit world? By going over the beads, our essence is changed. The next world is joined to ours. Maybe its essence is changed too. By contact with us. Wasn't Jesus a spirit who became man? Aren't our stories human that somehow transcend? Aren't both changed by both?

Aren't the beads just a symbol, then, of literature?

Are they also symbols of literary theory? Maybe they are literary theory. Well, you can see the problems in the transcendence of *lit thit*. Rolling around a long line of erasing boundaries.

Being nothing.

Being all.

Meanings forever disappearing and always there.

The new *multi-formality*. With its *accomplice-isity* to things. The necessary accomplice of the new ethnicity which is there too in the new literary theory. Discussing Native American literature in Native American terms.

Naming our own language with which to discuss.

Now there is movement and stopping between the reading and the writing of the reviews. Jumping not only from function to function but also between writing that is more essay or functional toward the more experimental. From concrete to abstract and back again. The first two reviews that follow are perhaps more functional. The third one belongs to the experimental.

# A Review of *Almanac of the Dead* by
# Leslie Marmon Silko

> You don't have anything
> if you don't have the stories.
> *Ceremony*, Leslie Silko

I've taught Silko's earlier work, *Ceremony*, for years. The Great American Indian Novel, in my opinion. The power of the sun now on earth. Since the 1945 dropping of the atomic bomb anyway. A new evil let loose and what can we do about it? That's the argument. Can old ceremonies work in the face of this new evil?

In *Ceremony*, Tayo returns from World War II as *The Wounded*. He's out of harmony with the earth. He cursed the rain when he was in the jungle and believes he is the cause of the drought in his homeland when he returns. Which is his major sickness. Along with Alcohol. Posttraumatic Stress Syndrome. Guilt. Others.

To be healed, (1) Tayo tells his story to a *new-style* Medicine Man, who makes a sand painting then cuts Tayo's head so blood will flow, (2) Tayo finds the Mexican cattle (acts, in other words), and (3) Tayo chooses not to do evil when his opportunity arises (he decides not to kill Emo when he has a chance). Therefore the beginning of the healing of *The Wounded*.

The major point of the book is that *story* is the beginning and continuum of healing. Or the process of story. Of adding your voice to the existing structure.

*Without a story you don't have anything.* Pretty ripe. Taking responsibility. Moving on.

171

But for me *Ceremony* (published in 1977) is still the classic statement on storytelling and its positive effect. It can heal where all else fails. It can also cause unbearable suffering.

Midway in *Ceremony* there's a chilling story of witches trying to impress one another with their stories. Finally one witch tells the story of the coming white man and the evils of war. *All right*, the others say, *you've got us beat. Now take that story back.* Of course she answers that she can't because once you speak, your words set the story in motion. What you say is what you get.

Maybe that's the entry to *Almanac of the Dead*. Since I don't know where else to begin.

From how to begin to live (your words make the trail on which you walk) to how to be dead. What's up in this oversized?

The table of contents alone is a trip. Divided into six parts with one to eight books in each part. The titles of the parts are peripatetic: *The U.S.A., Mex., Africa, The Americas, The Fifth World,* and *One World, Many Tribes.* The books within the parts are zoners: *Dried Up Corpse, Burning Children, Plane Crashes, Severed Heads, Tucson Witches, .44 Magnum Has Puppies, Cop Cakes,* and *Nude Cop Pinups* to spot a few.

The Spirit Snake's message in the book is that the world is about to end (p. 235).

Or, as Old Pancakes says, "The world that the whites brought with them would not last. It would be swept away in a giant gust of wind. All they had to do was to wait. It would be only a matter of time" (p. 235).

There are a lot of characters in *Almanac.*

A lot of pages.

Which begin with individual aging.

But actually the aging of an age.

The burden of time. From the old Mayan myth.

The approaching night. The West Pole.

The collapse of civilization.

The crumble.

Every description is society in the advanced stages of de-composition.

Many of the books within the novel are hard to read. Beaufry's films of abortion, sex-change operations, and the ritual circumcision of young girls, the scenes of global torture, even the whorehouses and drug scenes in the underworld of Tucson, are among the most chilling.

But what is this continual, confusing, crowded, self-indulgent, solipsistic, speaking-evil sort of life-force that Silko sets in motion? Why do I have to read this? Do I need to know the morbid, sick behavior of humanity in its decline?

And what if it isn't over yet? What if time goes on and I need positive storytelling and not wallowing in the evil that abounds?

Not a sentimental look back to the old days. But the quiet strength-force of my grandmother after another kind of people came and took our way of life. The power of words to sustain. Even in her silence she gave me words.

I still hear them though she's been gone nearly forty years.

Wallo.

Maybe there's something here I'm not getting. But I don't see it yet. And what do I think I should be learning? I think education is really love. It's the passing on of tools needed for survival. If the Native American thinks the old boarding schools were cruel, how about the stories of what the Indian elders did to the Indian children who fell asleep during the winter's storytelling? According to one account, a hole was cut in the ice and the child lowered so he would remember to stay awake during storytelling because knowing stories meant survival. The un-mythed (uneducated) mind was doomed. Unless it could retell, not verbatim, but including one's own voice in the story, so that the individual became whole on his migration. In his story-making.

So what lesson is Silko giving? Are we being *dunked?*

Your words are as close as your skin. Just as you have to be careful who you sleep with, you have to be careful what stories you tell. In the sexual union two people become one. Something happens we don't see with the eyes, nor understand, but somehow two things are joined. The child born is a symbol of the union. The Native American believes the same sort of process is started with words. (We are joined to what we say.) (Not all Native Americans believe the same thing, of course. Beliefs are as diverse as the people. So I should say, "Some Native Americans believe . . .") (Maybe "What I believe . . .")

Maybe *Almanac* is a typical Coyote trickster story and what it's really about will emerge somewhere down the road. Say next month when you're driving somewhere and the story comes back to your mind where it's been motoring all the time anyway and suddenly it parks and you know the meaning. The point behind the text. And you see the old Coyote heart beating under his chest. And you laugh because things are all right or not all right sometimes after all.

But for now.

"The first time Roy and Peaches fuck, Roy gets her so good she tells him about the arrangement between Bio-Materials and the human organ transplant industry across the U.S. The Japanese had developed a saline gel that kept human organs fresh-frozen and viable for transplant for months, not hours. Peaches did not explain where or how Trigg had obtained the human hearts and lungs carefully packed and clearly labeled: Type A Positive Adult Male.

"Frozen human organs, less reliable, sold for a fraction of freshly harvested hearts and kidneys. Of course, fetal brain-tissue and cadaver skin were not affected by freezing. Peaches said Trigg bought a great deal in Mexico where recent unrest and civil strife had killed hundreds a week. Mexican hearts were lean and strong but Trigg had found no market for dark cadaver skin" (p. 404).

There are important messages in *Almanac* among the passages about characters from the underworld:

"War had been declared the first day the Spaniards set foot on Native American soil, and the same war had been going on ever since: the war was for the continents called the Americas" (p. 133).

"'Leave our Mother Earth alone,' the old folks had tried to warn, 'otherwise terrible things will happen to us all'" (p. 759).

The warnings of uranium mines, the draining of the Ogalala Aquifer, the drying up of American cities. In the end, Silko feels the buffalo will return and the indigenous peoples who know how to live on an annual rainfall. Which seems improbable to me. But we need to hear these things. This book is prophetic warning. A gigantic look at our own horror. "A book written for us all," Joy Harjo has said.

In the March 14, 1995, *Saint Paul Pioneer Press*, there was a picture story called "Organs for Sale." The article read,

*The shantytown of Villivakkam near Madras, India, is famous for its cut-rate kidneys. A resident points to her friend's scar after a donation procedure. A peasant is typically paid $1000 for a kidney and scores of clinics are taking advantage of the lucrative market.*

I thought of *Almanac of the Dead* as I read the story. But the rest of the book? I'm not ready to go that far. It's still a matter of choice.

The image that sticks with me after I'm finished with *Almanac of the Dead*: "Buzzard was the king those years. You should have seen. They don't have to drink much water. They get it from the rotting meat they eat. It swells up with gas and then it makes greenish waters. Buzzards gather around and feast. It is like their beer. They drink and drink" (p. 202).

There was a place in the middle of the book where I got involved in the reading. But why do I have the label of *misuse of words* for *Almanac?*

I want to say *Make your words worthy of the page.*

Not some soap opera of the underworld.

I want to be cruel.

That's what the book does for me so far.

I want to say *buzzard beer.*

I want to give it to someone I don't like.

But there's more to it.

The broken story line, for instance. *The many voices telling the story too big to be told by one. The too little told because so much is known* type-of-hype we hear about Native writers.

This book affects me personally. It's a matter of ideology rather than blood, as it often is in the Native world. It forces my beliefs to the surface. My process of storytelling. The choices I have made. Is that what *Almanac* is about?

It puts responsibility on me. The book knocks on my head with the realization that we are in trouble here. Terrible things are happening in the world. I know they are happening. But I don't think I know what to do about them.

On the other hand, I'm angry about this book. The way in which it's told. I don't want this kind of life. I don't want to sink into the titillating "high" Rambo roll of drama in *Almanac.* Riding my Harley. Injecting Valvoline. A part of the Tex-Mex-Sex scene. I don't want to be whizzed through the quick orgasmic after-intake of drugs. I don't want this residue in my head. I want these characters to stop behaving that way. I don't want to read about them as characters at all. I don't want it to be believed that all Native people behave that way. I'm back to my own storytelling of life.

Maybe that's the life in *Almanac of the Dead.*

It forces me to rethink my own text. Again and again. To stand firmer in this late-age pinball downroll to the lowest point of civilization (though torture, scuzz, and the human behavior we read about in *Almanac* have always been with us). Reading this book brings me to some fundamental matters. The fact of evil that also comes out of humanity and I am part of it.

I want to take this anger that the book has provoked in me and say, "What's wrong on this earth?" I want to put on the brakes. But the trip takes me back to Sunday school in the Bible Belt when I was a child. And the Baptist and fundamental vacation Bible school teachers who said there is a heart of darkness in the world. There is darkness in the heart of me.

I am an accomplice. But there is also a book of life. And which was I going to choose? That's what *Almanac* does. Sends me to the Native American Mazakute Church I attend right now. Sends me to church in every place I ever lived. Back to the thought of the Christian religion and Jesus on the cross. Back to the appreciation of my parents who remained decent even when their lives were unhappy. They provided a home and education. They provided faith as a sanctuary that overcame evil. Even into the dark pages of *Almanac* full of unspeakable horrors. There is a way. There is a choice.

"Ck'o'yo magic won't work if someone is watching us," one of the witchmen says toward the end of *Ceremony*. Well, I want to be one who is watching.

The book also makes me afraid. I don't want it to pass into storytelling. Leave the words unspoken in the book. Read it under the covers with your flashlight. Look only at the body of the words (which are the written parts of the pages). Leave the spirit (the sound of the text) in the book. Maybe then it will have less power.

# Winter Recount: A Review of
## *Shadow Catcher* by Charles Fergus

A *shadow catcher* is a photographer. The term was used by many Native Americans, the givers of many words and concepts in our language. Along with staples such as corn. Potatoes. Already you know the bias of my review. A topical underpinning of this novel is the change from stiff nineteenth-century photography to candid shots. Taking people when they didn't know they were being photographed. It seemed at first there was something *sinful* to that. At least dangerous in Native terms. What happened to the photograph happened to you. There's even a photograph of Hopis hiding from the camera so a part of them wouldn't die. So their *shadow* wouldn't be caught. Charles Fergus is not a Native writer, but he does some Native writing in *Shadow Catcher*. He catches a people himself as they came to their *West Pole* and began to see themselves through the lens of another culture. At least it's a complex view. Adding dimension to the daguerreotype.

The novel is full of words and phrases and passages of clean, well-scrubbed prose. *The goiter, smooth and round, of a misplaced breast. The cramped arm of a canyon. White handkerchiefs that rise and fall like moths. A woman still as a doe in the brush.* Images like that stay with you. Fergus spent eight years in the research and writing of the book. You can feel the years.

The structure of the historical novel is the germination of an idea for an Indian statue in New York harbor to accompany the Statue of Liberty. To commemorate the Indian who was thought to be vanishing, though neither happened. A year later, in 1913, a *goodwill* expedition reached out to the Indians who hadn't quite managed to vanish. The historical event was the Rodman Wanamaker Train *Expedition of Citizenship to the*

*North American Indian.* To interest the Indians in the country that robbed them of their land and culture. To get them to become citizens and vote. *Bullshit,* someone calls from the audience. Nonetheless the expedition travels by rail to some seventy-five reservations across country. From Washington, D.C., west to Oklahoma, New Mexico, Arizona, California, the Northwest coast, and back through the Dakotas.

Accompanying the expedition is Ansel Fry, the *"street"* photographer. The book contains some thirty-three photographs from the trip. Most of them moving. *Boys being taught to sweep the porch at Riverside Indian School, Anadarko, Oklahoma. Pala sweat bath lodge. Night dedication of the flag to the Chickasaw Nation, Oklahoma. A Havasupai mother and child. Sitting Bull.* One photo (Custer's field, Montana) is simply landscape, half land, half sky. And look at the old face of Chief Red Cloud if you want to know what the defeat of acculturation was like.

Two "treaty" photographs, "Sitting Bear signing the Declaration of Allegiance to the U.S. Government" and especially "Signing the Declaration of Allegiance by Colville Reservation Indians," look like the Indians are being fingerprinted after arrest. Which gets closer to "the truth" than the idealized Wanamaker expedition interpretation of events.

Ansel Fry could take the stilted photographs we know from history. Any good photographer could "push the plate-holder into the camera's back. Disappear beneath the black cloth, fine-tune the focus, emerge, set the aperture, pull the slide out of the plate-holder, grasp the India-rubber bulb at the end of the cable. When the subjects and photographer were ready, the shutter was opened. Thousand one. Thousand two. Thousand three. After the count, the shutter eased shut. If anyone moved during the long process, their faces blurred." A process as tedious as the picture.

But Ansel Fry could also take the *real* photographs. Those

"Fruit of the Lens" and "The Camera: A Moral Force" kind-of-photographs. Those in which the subjects aren't stiff as the plate. He used a new camera. One small enough to be hidden in his coat. "It seemed almost weightless yet it held so much." Fry walks down the street. "His suit was gray. The vest had five black buttons. Unless a person were sharply observant, he would never notice that the middle button was different. It had a face of glass."

By the time of the Wanamaker expedition, Fry had polished his technique. "The oblique approach, the barest pause (head turned as if his attention were elsewhere), the subtle click, turning and moving away again, on the prowl."

Fergus called his book *"faction"* at his Hungry Mind Bookstore reading in St. Paul. The dialogue, of course, is *made up.* License is used with other matters. For the sake of historical drama. We take what we know and create the rest. We *recount the winter count, or "crate" and "recrate" events.* It's the best we can hope for in knowing what came before us.

The purpose Fergus had in writing his book: "We are all individuals both red and white and we should not be thought of as stereotypes." Okay (also an Indian word). Not one of us is good or bad altogether but a strange mixture of loose discord and concise disagreement. At least one of our five buttons is glass. In the end taking what we see best.

There are other people in the story: Joseph Dixon, Wanamaker's photographer, who romanticized the Native experience; James McLaughlin, the Indian agent, whose "real" memories of the arrest of Sitting Bull haunt Ansel Fry; Annie Owns the Fire, McLaughlin's adopted daughter, who joins the expedition after she is fired from Carlisle Indian School for teaching about the Sun Dance and talking Indian language. There're other kinds of memorials than photography: conversations, written records, ceremonies, monuments.

Some of McLaughlin's words:

"The members of Sitting Bull's band sat in chairs around the room—
a collection of more savage faces I had never seen. One man wore
welders' goggles with one of the lenses missing. Another had on a
bloodstained railroader's cap. A third wore a dozen scalps sewn to
his shirt. Another had a necklace of dried toads. . . . I thought I had
calmed myself, but when I looked into those black, hateful eyes, my
stomach tensed and my gorge rose."

The agents go on to tell Sitting Bull that "the Great Father
thinks the biggest chief is the Indian who learns the white man's
ways. The Indian who plants crops and builds his own house. Who
learns to live by the sweat of his brow. Who goes to the white man's
church. Who sends his children to school. You and your people will
receive your fair share of the goods and supplies that come to this
agency for distribution. . . . The Great Father has sent me to take
care of you and to labor in your behalf. I hold the same relation to
you that a father holds toward his children. And, as the first thing
that is required on the part of the children is obedience, so must
you willingly obey me and follow my commands." I didn't mean
to quote so much, but it's hard to stop . . . "You will not leave the
vicinity of the agency without permission. The use of alcohol is
strictly forbidden. . . . Look around you. The game is almost gone.
In a few years the buffalo will be gone and you will no longer see
the footprints of the deer."

Annie Owns the Fire's thoughts are also poignant:

The land glowed in the starlight. She heard the horses ripping out
grass and grinding it. Stars everywhere, coming down to the horizon,
a sudden scratch of fire as a meteor abraded to nothingness. She let her
head rest in the pocket between two spokes. The stars begin to swim, to
run together, all the little flecks of brilliance swirling and melting like
a rage of windblown snow. She lowered her face and wept.

The weight of these kinds of truths eventually may bring
America to its own "West Pole."

And there're many other issues in the book: what is real ver-
sus what is imagined.

"Fry walked down a path to where an old man lay snoring before a hovel of boards and brush, his face puffy as an apple left out through too many frosts. Fry let his coat fall open. Placing his hand in his pocket, he set himself and took the picture.

"The Apaches! In grade school he had written a report on them. On the frontispiece of the source book was an engraving of an Apache warrior, a lean, bandy-legged man in a pale shirt and breechcloth—the toughest most merciless fighter in the world—"

What was this Fry was seeing with his camera? How could his Apache in the schoolbook and the one before him on the ground be the same? What was truth and what was illusion? How could the camera convey both? Did the images cancel one another? What were the implications?

There are more questions of reality. When Dixon, for instance, pays a woman at a loom to pose for a picture she doesn't want to. While she is sitting for the picture, Fry takes a candid picture of Dixon taking the staged picture. Like one of those mirrored galleries where the image goes on and on. "A photograph of a photograph: an image stolen of an image bribed: an instant frozen from separate points of view."

In the end, no one viewpoint emerges, but it's how we see—that's the Native American concept of things.

The problem of establishing meaning within a text points to some contemporary concerns from a historical setting. The impossibility of connecting shifting signifiers and *signifieds*. Defining photography in the same context of, well, stripping the well-meaning image from its intended object. Or of attempting to solidify the moving world into the portrait of a nearly impossible still life. It's the quandary of any sign-maker.

"I took forbidden pictures. I drew a bead on truth," Fry says. "I stole souls." What else can the writer or photographer hope to do?

# Emergent Literatures That Challenge the Standard; or, Mammy Yokum *hollerin bout sumthun*

Native American Theater. Spiderwoman Theater. I saw it last Saturday night. The women started slowly unraveling the tension buildup of the usual. The expected conflict/climax/resolution. Intertwined it with patience. Take time. Where this going? Oh. Slow dance. Flute play. Poke. Poke. This a story? No. But *stery*. A history turned *herstory* turned *herstery*. A *sterying*. Mammy Yokum at the backyard kettle.

Now beat drum. Oh. Oh. Only men beat drum. Whad these women? But a form of *herstery*. Women's new theater without its bounds. I almost said without its hands. Without the dominant text of its authority.

Iconoclast. A series of surdramas. Not *sir*. Nosir. By no means. But beyond drama. The borders of what had been new ground. Women looking at themselves. All saying their voices.

Laughing at themselves. At Indian enrollment. At a lot of things.

Now, in one scenelet. The ground of what it is to be a mouse eaten by the owl. How to be called from the nest-hole on a moonlit Saturday night. How the mouse comes into the field of her aria. Lured by the darkness and the moonbeams showing themselves. She too is called. On a trajectory of her longing. How she offers her little foot. How the owl woos her as if loved for herself and not the source she provides. To get owleaten is her privilege. Her recognition of how-to-be. Her right. According to owl. She nestles in the nightgrass and the owl chows her. Chow. We know. Weno.

I *seen* these two shepherds walking down the street after school. One of these warm October afternoons that last about as long as a mouse in the field. With the owl overhead thinking bingo.

*Wallo.* They walk walk going somewhere for something. One boy with a white towel over his head and a staff in his hand. The other a shepherd too. Though not so shepherdy.

Looking at them, I would say theater is a shepherd in the context of sheep. No, to change the mind, I would say that theater is an owl *on the look* for a mouse. Calling it softly in a performance of the kill. When you leave yourself and enter the stery. When you are absorbed by it. Taken into it. Forgetting yourself until you do not exist. Except in the stomach of the owl. A real Jonah story. My own thought processes annihilated for a while. And even afterwards not a whole part of myself again. So changed by the surdrama.

The lugubrious and turgid voices. AAAAAAaaaaaaaaa.

Deconstructed in the beak of the text.

*Just do it quickly,* I say.

Words create. Yet to speak destroys.

I think to take invisibility and to take new. To cut up pieces like quilt-scraps-making and something different. It's the spider who said *weave,* you know.

The hands painted on the buckskin dress, for instance. The Ghost Dance looking beyond. When the end comes into being. The squeezing through the invisible because there's no way back.

The problem with a Native script is that it forces you into yourself. To hear your own voice calling but act like you don't.

Now thiz iz the herstery. Which becomes really yeurstery. Another view. An *undune obsequium.* Blueprints. Handprints. The difference in concept between.

The herstery has to dream. Has to come alive. Has to restery the womb of the ear. If it were a focused life script we would miss.

A birch bark scroll in which there are four rooms and the entrant enters and walks through. Past the things that hold her back the things that send her forward hope despair all that Ghost Dance–studded stuff and how to make a journey of it past hindrances and *himdrances* and whatever *herdrances* you know yourself as dragging your *feetprints*.

And there in the one line calling for many. The left out community defining itself in *stery*. Getting the construct of a physical object by a mental assembling plant line.

More doing than saying I'm doing because to speak is to drive the sheep away so you make a sound and it sounds how if you examine something it disappears.

The voice that can't always speak but rides on words.

Talking one thing to mean another.

A dream within a dream.

A dream's dream dreaming.

A shepherd shepherding or an owl owling.

In the end, Mammy Yokum *hollerin bout sumthun*.

So what comes of it? Other than vitality validity the wholeness of the hole of ignored voices. A composite scene. A more balanced balance.

It's a theater I'm telling the accrual of words.

My ears have nests, you know.

The owl eats.

Yum.

NOW

# Hereafter

I'm just past fifty, you see. Maybe I've lived most of it. I think
this morning when I wake and don't have to get up what it will
be. There's the idea of chairs, probably in rows. And ever so
often you say *Hallelujah.* Or *Glory to you, heavenly hosts. Father, Son, and Holy Ghost.* Mostly I think Jesus gets the attention. But in the prairie grass of my heart I see my father waiting
for me. Because I loved him most. We say *hallo.* I hear the buffalo snort. I hear the migration again. It's so quiet you know.
Unlike the buffalo who rumble the place. But the Plains Indian
migration is just some feet walking on the earth. Some horses
pulling travois. A few camp dogs loaded with their little packs.
Maybe your grandmother humming. Nothing that would
quicken your ear if you were standing say a hundred yards
away. But this might be what the hereafter is like. It's what the
Ghost Dancers said anyway. The Hunting Grounds stretch
through the universe. Just more of the Great Plains. In fact, the
Milky Way is a map of migration. The spiral path. *Glory to you,
Heavenly Ghosts.* And you look up and there's your great-great-
great-grandpa you never knew, of course, and you can ask him
how it was in his day and you tell him how it was in yours. Yes,
and you can hold it all together the way the seers can. The way
the medicine men told you in their visions. And you say *Wow
it's true.* All those things you couldn't see. Didn't understand.
The trappings trapped. The small-sightedness cleared out. You
see the heavenly grazing ground. Just like you do across South
Dakota. You see justice. And his name is Christ. But he's not
the spirit you hoped he was. But a living being. A man with a
white buckskin breechcloth and moccasins on his feet and a

bow across his shoulder. His face is marked with war. One half painted black. The other yellow. And you say *Hallelujah*. And he rides over the heavenly fields and comes to a corral of bitterness you brought and shoots into it. You see it's really the parts of you that are different from him. And you say *Glory to you Chief Christ*. And he takes his tomahawk and scalps the fear from your heart. That hairy part you're better off without. And you see as he sees. And you never knew anyone like him. You see the Hunting Grounds. You hear the pow wow drum just like you were in Sisseton, South Dakota. And you see the big chair of heaven. Well, there are chairs. Rows and rows of them. For those who called *Christ*. The unforgivable sin is not believing. If you want in God's heaven. Because then you don't have a raffle ticket to win the star-quilt. Who would have thought? None of us could have madethatup. It wasn't what you did on earth, but what you believed. And if you just said *Christ* the moment you died, you were there. *Wow*. Maybe with less than others who always believed. Maybe some with no horse or rifle. Maybe only a piece of flint so you could start your fire. But it's always light. What do you need a fire for anyway? The many-buffalo feast is just there. No hunting. Scraping. All that work. You don't have to do it anymore. It's just a pow wow all through forever. You know how sometimes you wanted it to go on and on. You wanted it never to be over. You wanted to stomp your feet and never grow tired and feel like you were Indian again.

# *Seated Bird Man*, Leonard Boskin, Minneapolis Institute of Arts

Okay. This is about a guy whose arms are empty sockets. And where's his wings? He has legs but no toes. Only claws and a head with a beak. His body is a man's. But something like feathers are fingered into the bronze. No, he's not a bird, but a man in some sort of transition. He doesn't know what's ahead. He doesn't know what death is like, or the afterlife. Has he already died and is waiting to hear if he will get wings? Which is a reward. One of them. Is the afterlife a row of dorm beds? An open sky? Will he still have a heart he can feel heavy as the last potato in the sack? Is death something like the tunnel life comes through? No wonder he looks mad. Already he's so changed. What will creep up next? The biggest trip of all and zip. There're guidebooks if he goes to Pittsburgh. If he wants to cross Kansas, say. Points of interest. Average temps. But imagine. The final trip and he can't take anything. He doesn't know where he's going. There's no one he can rely on. Not in the Aristotelian reality-he-can-hold-in-his-hand anyway. And how does he get there? Maybe he just hitchhikes. Out behind the galaxy there'a a place he thumbs a ride. Maybe the stars are really the exhaust of traffic flying straight out of the solar system at night. Maybe wings will unfold from his back. It just takes a little faith and patience. Maybe he'll only run in circles like leaves outside the door. Particles of his spirit nothing more than cosmic dust. Or is the bird man waiting to hear if there's a bed made up for his arrival? Shoes neatly together. A marine barracks where he's partners like shoes with someone he didn't like on earth. Maybe he hasn't got it down yet. Maybe he already held out his hand, thumb up for a ride, and got his arm taken off. Then he tried it again. And now he's waiting armless at some airfield for a ticket. Waiting for his tour across America. Heading west, of course. Then off the edge of California, lifting unsteadily over the Pacific before turning to space.

# The New War Horse Is the Exercise Bike

A one-wheeled Schwinn resting on posts.
When I was a girl I had a two-wheeled Schwinn,
an American Flyer or something like that
I got on my eighth birthday.
I learned to ride it on the front walk.
Eventually I could ride it up the hill,
around the block,
to the schoolyard five blocks away.

Now I don't leave the room.

The new war horse has a book stand.
I can read now while I ride,
though it's through bifocals
the way I used to look through a magnifying glass
at leaves and rocks—
the whole universe of imagination.

The pedals sound like the old push lawn mower
forever past the flowers on my bedroom wall
always in bloom
even when the yard is covered with snow.

I ride until I feel like I'm getting somewhere.
I ride until I feel like a girl pow wow dancing.

You know how it is early in spring
when you get the yard raked up
and the rest of the afternoon is your own.
You can dream up anything.

Maybe that's what we're born for. To move toward this.

# He Has More Than One Ear

> He can hear many voices at once.
> If you get past the crowd
> and the fizz
> like steam on a sound stage of a rock concert
> you can see he is covered with ears.
>
> He who planted the ear, shall he not hear?
> Psalm 94:9

In a sweat lodge ceremony, a man was praying in Lakota. I don't understand his language and he prayed a long time and my mind wandered to my own concerns. The sweat lodge is a hot, dark *church* where we come together to pray for others. Sometimes ourselves. And I wondered if my separate thoughts got in the way of the Lakota man and the Great Spirit, and I thought no, the Great Spirit has more than one ear.

If he's like the Native culture, he prefers many narrators, many possibilities of meaning as he listens to his people struggle for reconnection, most of us without a manual.

To put my finger on something illusive, I've been thinking about Native American literature and culture and what they have to offer because I'm nearing the end of another semester and I think how can students understand the diverse culture? Full of strength and weakness. Meaning and no meaning. A people gone far away from themselves. A people zoned on themselves.

In the end, it's the moving variables that move again the moment you focus. It's transformation that is the constant.

That's what you get out of Native American literature and

culture after the life principles of harmony, reciprocity, balance, respect
after the presence of ancestors and the spirit world
after the interdependency of the group
after seeing the earth as a living being
after story and language as creator and maintainer
after a culture moving according to natural patterns
instead of linear organization
after another way of seeing
another way of being
in the end
what Native American literature and culture offer you is yourself
because in the end *you* have to define meaning
and it's what you are that you see.

Gerald Vizenor calls it the *tabernacle of mirrors* in his book *Dead Voices*. Not God's tabernacle in the wilderness with its ark of the covenant, but your own humanity—naked, uncomfortable, burdened, complex, unadaptable, contradictory, angry, humorous, arrogant, self-centered, generous.

Native American literature and culture offer you the seventh direction after North, East, South, West, Earth, Sky
there's Center
which is the core of yourself
you carry with you wherever you go.

# If Not All These

What's it like to pass from this world?

Is it a tunnel with a light at the end? A field in which your father waits and you talk to him again? Is it a drop into a well? A step you forgot was there jarring your teeth? Possibly death is a long trail to the far corner of the prairie. Sometimes wolves still howl.

Maybe death is a structure of language outside the voice. A getting-out-of-the-body like the chores you never wanted to do.

Here comes death wearing a white hat and a Lone Ranger mask.

Or an acquaintance whose name you can't remember when it's time to introduce him. Maybe death is riding a horse for the first time and not getting thrown.

A burst of gladiolas from an amphora.

Could death be the laundry chute in the old house where you sent your overalls? Even the cat.

Maybe it's the dust bowl. Or lunar desolation. The edge of the highway from which you can't step back.

Maybe death is a morning when you wake and remember it's your birthday. No—the first day of school you dreaded but find it's not so bad. And soon you get into it. You put on your pinwheel skirt. Your halo like an old propeller beanie. You flap your Teflon wings and soon you're far above the Rio Grande.

# Publication History

"Hides" and "Genealogy" first appeared in *Returning the Gift: Poetry and Prose from the First North American Native Writers' Festival*, edited by Joseph Bruchac, University of Arizona Press, Tucson, 1994.

"Culture and Environment: Voices in the Wind" first appeared in *Colors Magazine: Minnesota's Journal of Opinion by Writers of Color*, Minneapolis, Spring, 1993.

"Speaking the Corn into Being" first appeared in *Freeing the First Amendment: Critical Perspectives on Freedom of Expression*, edited by Robert Jensen and David Allen, copyright New York University Press, 1995. Reprinted by permission.

"The Woman Who Made Eyes" first appeared in *Poets at Work, Contemporary Poets—Lives, Poems, Process*, just buffalo literary center, Buffalo, New York, 1995.

"Snow," "Comanche," "You're Responsible for Your Own Leaves," "War Horse I," "War Horse II," and "War Horse III" appeared as the 1994 Winter Book, also called *The West Pole*, published by the Minnesota Center for the Book Arts.

"Short Flight from Minneapolis to Chicago" first appeared in *Untitled*.

"The Drinking Vessel" first appeared in *Pleiades*.

"Columbus Meets Thelma and Louise" first appeared in the *Women's Review of Books*, Wellesley College, Wellesley, Mass., July 1992.

"Sugar Woman" first appeared in *Without Discovery,* an anthology edited by Ray Gonzales, Blue Moon Press, Seattle, 1992.

"War Horse II" and "If Not All These" appeared in *The Party Train: An Anthology of North American Prose Poems,* edited by Robert Alexander, Mark Vinz, and C. W. Truesdale, New Rivers Press, Minneapolis, 1996.

Review of *Almanac of the Dead* first appeared in the *Hungry Mind Review,* St. Paul, Minnesota, May 1992.

"Winter Recount" first appeared in *City Pages: The Alternative News and Arts of the Twin Cities,* December 4, 1991.

"Seated Bird Man" first appeared in *The West Pole,* a collection of thirteen poems that won the 1990 *The And Review* poetry chapbook prize competition.

"He Has More Than One Ear" first appeared in *SAIL (Studies in American Indian Literatures): A Journal of Literary Art, Criticism, and Reviews,* Summer 1995

*Diane Glancy* is an associate professor at Macalester College in St. Paul, Minnesota, where she teaches Native American literature and creative writing. *The West Pole* is her second collection of essays. Her first collection, *Claiming Breath*, won the 1991 Native American Prose Award and a 1993 American Book Award. It was published in 1992 by the University of Nebraska Press. Glancy's first novel, *Pushing the Bear*, about the 1838 Removal of the Cherokee from the southeast to Oklahoma, was published in 1996. A second novel, *The Only Piece of Furniture in the House*, also was published in 1996. Glancy has received many awards, including grants from the National Endowment for the Arts, the National Endowment for the Humanities, and the Minnesota State Arts Board. She received an M.F.A. degree from the University of Iowa.